"THIS BOOK . . . is based on the experience of a lifetime devoted to the study of drawings with passionate enthusiasm. . . . In so vast a field the attempt has been made to select only examples that will fascinate and please the general reader." See Foreword, by Paul J. Sachs.

As a brilliant author, teacher, and administrator, Paul J. Sachs is one of the most respected figures in the art world. For many years, he was active at the Fogg Museum in Cambridge, Mass. During that period he acquired one of the finest collections of drawings in the world. As Professor of Fine Arts at Harvard University, Dr. Sachs profoundly influenced many of the young men who are now curators in the various museums of this country.

ARTISTS

whose works are reproduced in this book—their schools and dates

PREHISTORIC

Caves at Lascaux, So. France	30,000 to	17,000 B.C.

GREEK ISLAND OF RHODES

The Pistoxenos Painter	470	460 B.C.

CHINESE

Wu Chên	1280	1354

ITALIAN SCHOOL

Pisanello, Antonio	c1395	1455
Pollaiuolo, Antonio	c1432	1498
Signorelli, Luca	c1441?	1523
Verrocchio, Andrea del	1435	1488
Botticelli, Sandro	1444?	1510
Mantegna, Andrea	1431	1506
Bonsignori, Francesco	c1453	1519
Messina, Antonello da	c1430	1479?
Lippi, Filippino	c1457	1504
Leonardo da Vinci	1452	1519
Michelangelo	1475	1564
Perugino, Pietro	1446	1523
Raphael	1483	1520
Titian	c1477	1576
Tintoretto, Jacopo Robusti	1518	1594
Veronese, Paolo	1528	1588
Tiepolo, G. B.	1696	1770

GERMAN SCHOOL

Schongauer, Martin	c1445	1491
Master of the House Book	late 15th century	
Dürer, Albrecht	1471	1528
Grünewald, Matthias	c1465	1528
Grien, Hans Baldung	c1480?	1545
Holbein, Hans, the Younger	1497	1543

FLEMISH SCHOOL

Van Eyck, Jan	c1390	1441
Van der Weyden, Rogier	c1399	1464
Bruegel, Pieter, the Elder	c1520?	1569
Rubens, Peter Paul	1577	1640
Van Dyck, Anthony	1599	1641

DUTCH SCHOOL

Leyden, Lucas van	c1494?	1533
Rembrandt van Rijn	1606	1669

FRENCH SCHOOL

Fouquet, Jean	c1420	c1480
Clouet, François	1520?	1572
Poussin, Nicolas	c1594	1665
Claude Lorrain	1600	1682
Watteau, Jean Antoine	1684	1721
Boucher, François	1703	1770
Fragonard, Jean Honoré	1732	1806
Ingres, J. A. D.	1780	1867
Gericault, Theodore	1791	1824
Delacroix, Eugene	1798	1863
Corot, Camille	1796	1875
Millet, Jean François	1814	1875
Daumier, Honoré	1808	1879
Degas, Edgar	1834	1917

SPANISH SCHOOL

Goya, Francesco	1746	1828

THE POCKET BOOK OF GREAT DRAWINGS

By PAUL J. SACHS

WASHINGTON SQUARE PRESS, INC.

THE POCKET BOOK OF GREAT DRAWINGS

1961

Permission to quote from the following publications is gratefully acknowledged:

The Drawings of the Florentine Painters, Bernard Berenson. The University of Chicago Press, 1938.

Drawings by Michelangelo for the Libyan Sibyl, Bryson Burroughs, in The Metropolitan Museum of Art "Bulletin," Volume 22. Copyright, 1925.

Leonardo da Vinci: An Account of His Development as an Artist, Kenneth Clark, Cambridge University Press, England, 1939.

Raphael's Drawings, Ulrich Middeldorf. H. Bittner and Company, New York, 1945. Copyright, 1949, by Henry Regnery Company, Chicago.

One Hundred Master Drawings, edited by Agnes Mongan. Harvard University Press. Copyright, 1949, by the President and Fellows of Harvard College.

The Language of Drawing and Painting, Arthur Pope. Harvard University Press. Copyright, 1929, 1931, 1949, by the President and Fellows of Harvard College.

A History of European and American Sculpture, Chandler R. Post. Harvard University Press. Copyright, 1921, by the President and Fellows of Harvard College.

Rembrandt, Jakob Rosenberg. Harvard University Press. Copyright, 1948, by the President and Fellows of Harvard College.

Vasari's Lives of the Artists, Giorgio Vasari. By permission of Simon and Schuster, publishers. Copyright, 1946, by Betty Burroughs.

Designed by Maxwell Marxe

L

Published by
Washington Square Press, Inc.: Executive Offices, 630 Fifth Avenue; University Press Division, 32 Washington Place, New York, N.Y.

WASHINGTON SQUARE PRESS editions are distributed in the U.S. by Affiliated Publishers, Inc., 630 Fifth Avenue, New York 20, N.Y.

CONTENTS

LIST OF ILLUSTRATIONS

FOREWORD

THIS BOOK, IN SO FAR AS THE ALL IMportant matter of the choice of Great Drawings for reproduction is concerned, is based on the experience of a lifetime devoted to the study of drawings with passionate enthusiasm, and in collecting several hundred examples for the Fogg Museum of Art, Harvard University. In so vast a field the attempt has been made to select only examples that will fascinate and please the general reader. Most of the books listed under Recommended Reading, as well as the Portfolios cited, contain many more instructive reproductions.

The text is based on lectures delivered at the Lowell Institute, Boston; at the Sorbonne, Paris; at the Courtauld Institute, London, and at the Universities of Berlin and Bonn; as well as at Harvard University during thirty-six happy years.

A number of descriptive sentences are taken from the *Catalogue of Drawings in the Fogg Museum of Art* (Harvard University Press) first produced by Agnes Mongan and by me in 1940.

For the specialist a book like this can have only a limited interest. It is intended, primarily, for the novice who has curiosity about drawings and for the general reader, as a brief introduction to a fascinating field, in the hope that he may be stimulated to look at the expanding collections of Master Drawings in American museums, for no reproduction can ever do complete justice to an original. The book is intended to give the observant reader a helpful basis for understanding the language of the draughtsman through the scrutiny of fine examples. This then is little more, shall we say, than a springboard. I have yielded to the temptation, now and again, to enliven the narrative with the kind of story that any collector might tell about drawings that he has loved.

As the number of reproductions had to be limited, a rigorous selection was mandatory. So limited a choice inevitably reveals the taste of the author. Specific explanatory comments are introduced in the hope that their cumulative effect will make it clear why the title –Great Drawings–was adopted. There has been no attempt to write a survey of the history of art in terms of Drawings. Such surveys may be found in many excellent manuals. A few of the more recent are listed in the Recommended Reading.

Any experienced student of drawings will appreciate the fact that this book should not be looked upon as an Anthology of reproductions of drawings from a technical or historical point of view. For such an exacting task, many more reproductions would be required and in that case there would have been included, to mention only a few Italian masters, additional Great

Drawings by such artists as:—Fra Angelico, Benozzo Gozzoli, Uccello, Ghirlandaio, Andrea del Sarto, the Bellini, Carpaccio, Guardi, Canaletto, and a dozen others; in the Netherlands:—Bouts, Memling, Hugo van der Goes, Bosch, and the Dutch landscape artists of the seventeenth century; in England:—Blake, Gainsborough, Constable and Turner; in Germany, Altdorfer and Cranach; in France and among artists identified with France:—David, Chasseriau, Rousseau, Daubigny, Guys, Renoir, Manet, Cézanne, Seurat, Van Gogh, Toulouse-Lautrec and Picasso, as well as a certain number of Americans.

To cover the modern and contemporary field, a separate volume is needed.

This book would never have been written but for the encouragement of my friend and former pupil, Herman Wechsler, whose attractive *Pocket Book of Old Masters* served as a model and prompted me to try something similar, in this limited fashion, in the field of drawings.

My indebtedness is very real to my connoisseur friends W. G. Russell Allen and Carl E. Pickhardt, Jr., for discussing with interest and patience the final selection of drawings. Grateful acknowledgment is also made for help received from Kojiro Tomita and W. G. Constable, both of the Museum of Fine Arts, Boston; Professor C. A. Robinson of Brown University; and to my former colleagues at the Fogg Museum—Agnes Mongan, Arthur Pope, Chandler R. Post, and Jakob Rosenberg—who have generously allowed me to quote passages from their books. The same is true of Bernard Berenson, Sir Kenneth Clark, Professors

Ulrich Middeldorf, Meyer Schapiro and Jean Seznec.

I express sincere thanks and appreciation for bibliographical and other assistance to such dear friends as Louise Lucas, Librarian, and her assistants Mary Ward and Helen Styles, as well as to Helen Willard, Elaine Evans and Ruth Magurn of the Departments of Drawing and of Prints; to James Ufford, photographer, and to Mary Wadsworth, my former devoted secretary. These friends are all on the staff of the Fogg Museum.

Mrs. Anne Blake Freedberg, Mrs. Anselm Beal, and Mrs. Robert Bogart have been patient in typing the manuscript.

To others who have given me kind suggestions, I express sincere thanks and appreciation.

I owe my deepest gratitude to my ever patient wife.

Grateful acknowledgment for permission to use copyrighted material is made to the various publishers, and appears under "Acknowledgments."

Indebtedness for photographs is acknowledged in the "List of Illustrations."

Paul J. Sachs

CAMBRIDGE, MASS.
FEBRUARY 1, 1951

TO THE MEMORY OF ROYAL CORTISSOZ

"The world is divided, for me, into two groups, formed respectively of those who care for drawings and those who do not. For those who do care there is nothing so thrilling as a good drawing. I have ridden this hobby all my life and I know."

PREHISTORIC
CAVES
30,000 to
17,000 B.C.
THE STAG
FRIEZE
Lascaux,
So. France

Plate 1

THE PISTOXENOS PAINTER

Greek Island of Rhodes, 470 · 460 B.C.

APHRODITE ON A GOOSE

British Museum, London

WU CHÊN

Chinese, 1280 · 1354

BAMBOO IN THE WIND

Museum of Fine Arts, Boston

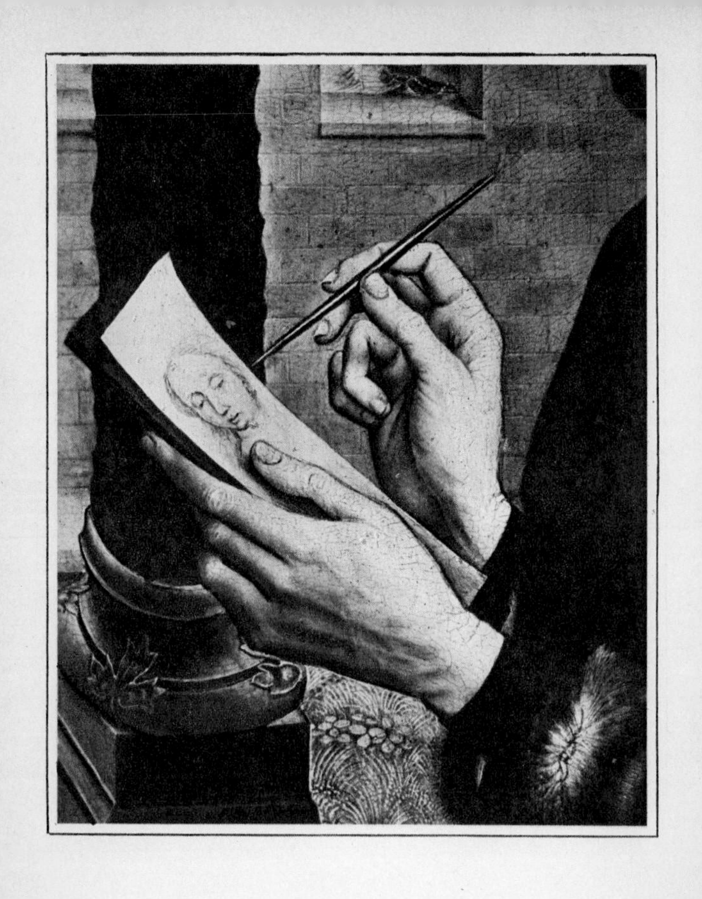

ROGIER VAN DER WEYDEN

c. 1399 · 1464

ST. LUKE DRAWING THE VIRGIN *(detail)*

Pinakothek, Munich

Plate 4

PISANELLO

c.1395 · 1455

TWO STUDIES OF A HORSE

Louvre, Paris

POLLAIUOLO

c.1432 · 1498

ADAM

Uffizi, Florence

Plate 6

SIGNORELLI

c.1441? · 1523

NUDE MAN AND KNEELING NUDE WOMAN

British Museum, London

Plate 7

VERROCCHIO

1435 · 1488

HEAD OF A WOMAN

Christ Church, Oxford

Plate 8

I

VARIOUS TYPES *of* DRAWING

A Background

MY STUDENTS OFTEN ASKED ME AT A first meeting:—What is a drawing? How are drawings made? What is a great drawing?

The word "draw" means:—to drag a pen or other instrument over a surface which leaves a mark behind it. To draw is to outline; to delineate; to represent a form or shape by lines or by means of light and shade alone or within a simple outline:—in short, to make a picture by such means. An artist's line has fundamental significance when it reveals form or design.

Everybody has made drawings of sorts, either at school, making white lines with chalk on a blackboard, or, as grownups, making dark lines on paper while "doodling" at desk or telephone. Such drawings are, of course, at the very opposite pole from great drawings, even if there is the enchanting legend that an Italian shepherd boy, in maturity the genius Giotto (1266?-1337), was discovered by the great artist, Cimabue (1240-1302), sketching his sheep while tending them.

Almost everyone can learn to speak correctly, to

write passably. Since writing is, after all, a kind of drawing, it follows that most people do draw. But, merely to write simple messages or to speak sentences does not make you a poet or an orator—a Shakespeare or a Churchill.

To draw lines or outlines is a way to express ideas—the grammar of art. Drawing is, indeed, the fundamental element in all great picture making, just as grammar is at the root of all good writing.

Good drawings have been produced by many men and women of talent, but, as in the case of author, poet, musician or orator, only a genius can produce a *great* work of art of any kind, a great drawing which, in addition to skillful handling, instantly brings to us the thought, the emotion of the artist at the time of creation.

I hope that the pictures and comments in these pages will help to supply the answers to the three questions, in greater detail, and that this *basic language* of great draughtsmen will become comprehensible, for it is in his drawings that the artist makes his most spontaneous statements, and enables us to follow his thought in the very act of creation. Long before Ingres, one of the remarkable draughtsmen of the nineteenth century, insisted that drawing is the probity of art, Vasari had said in the sixteenth century:— "drawing . . . is the necessary beginning of everything [in art], and not having it one has nothing."

My pet slogan is what it has always been:— the eye is best trained through an intimate knowledge of the best. Understanding and discrimination, that is, "connoisseurship," can only be developed by repeated contact with the best visual images produced in the draughtsman's *own* language. How, if we continue to rely chiefly on those who would lull us with fine words, can we hope to *see*.

The instinct for *quality* has made for the success of the great collectors. They have, as a rule, relied upon their direct reaction to the isolated object. Often they have preceded, indeed formed, the critics. The drawings selected for reproduction in this book are not chosen because of their rarity, but because, whether slight, quick sketches or finished designs, they give evidence, through their technical excellence, of the translation of the vision of the artist into graphic language. For the beginner it is the training of the eye which counts. The eye is best trained through an intimate knowledge of the best. A brief account of how drawings are made should prove helpful.

• • •

In *Prehistoric Times*, a sharpened stone was probably employed to cut a design on a bone. The result:— a drawing. The earliest types of distinguished drawings known to us are prehistoric, spirited drawings discovered on the walls of rock shelters or caves. These prehistoric caves contain vivid representations of animals —among others, wild horses, stags, bison, and *reindeer*, (Plate 1),—as well as hunters. Such caves were decorated from seventeen thousand to thirty thousand or more years ago. The caves at Lascaux, in the Valley of the Dordogne, in Southern France, were discovered by two French schoolboys, during World War II. These caves are believed to have been sanctuaries and the pictures that decorate them, though probably older, are comparable in importance only to those at Altamira in Northern Spain. The Altamira pictures were made known to the world years ago by careful copies. The reproductions of the Lascaux pictures were made from beautiful photographs taken by Fernand Windels, to whom we are grateful for a thoroughly trustworthy record of this amazing paleolithic art. We surmise that these cave pictures were produced not so much with decoration in mind, but rather that they illustrate prehistoric man's belief in the magic power of picture making; a help in dominating his prey. While as a rule these prehistoric, symbolic cave pictures represent more or less isolated animals or figures; the one that we illustrate has an added interest in that the animals are related to each other, in sequence, in a frieze fifteen feet in length.

Many readers will recall the color photographs of these pictures that appeared in *Life* shortly after their discovery and which are now beautifully published by the Viking Press.

• • •

Since almost all traces of wall painting have perished, our knowledge of *Greek painting* is derived chiefly from vases which were produced in large numbers at Corinth, Athens and other city-states during classical times and were used most frequently as mixing bowls, flasks, or receptacles for water, wine, oil, or as drinking cups.

We are fascinated by the clean outline, the happy decorative effect in the exquisite example from the Greek island of Rhodes, of *Aphrodite on a Goose* (Plate 2), attributed to the workshop of the Pistoxenos painter, active about 470-460 B.C. The figure is perfectly adapted to the circular space. One does not have to be a specialist in the history of Greek vases to appreciate its distinction. We shall find nothing more exquisite in the pages that follow.

• • •

In the *Bamboo in the Wind*, a *Chinese work* (Plate 3), both the picture and the fine calligraphy were produced by Wu Chên, a celebrated fourteenth century artist. Observe that the Bamboo is superbly represented with one main stalk and several branches stirred in the wind. In China such masterly wash drawings were made with ink and brush with magic dexterity and exquisite restraint. Mr. Kojiro Tomita, the Curator of Oriental Art at the Museum of Fine Arts, Boston, has kindly translated the delightful inscription in these words:—

> "The bamboo is not originally endowed with mind,
> Yet its thought seems to soar into the clouds.
> Quietly standing in the lonesome mountain
> Dignified, typifying the will of a gentleman.
> Mei Tao—[Wu Chên] playfully painted and wrote."

This one example from China should serve as a reminder that in certain fields we of the West have everything to learn from the East. To get such an apparently simple but miraculous result as this there must be no retouching. *Brush* technique demands the kind of rigorous training that Chinese artists knew and to which few in the West have ever been subjected.

• • •

Returning now to Europe and coming down to the fifteenth and early sixteenth centuries, we find that draughtsmen used sharp instruments to record their ideas.

Silver point, the favorite tool used by artists in Italy, in the Netherlands, and sometimes in Germany, yields delightful delicate results. The artist coated his parchment or paper with a thin colored ground of powdered bone, mixed with gum water, drawing upon it as the ingenious and graceful Florentine, Filippino Lippi (Plate 13), did in the fifteenth century. The result is a pale gray line which is attractive by virtue of its crispness and clarity. Unity is here achieved because of the harmony between the sharp, sensitive stroke of Lippi's drawing and the delicately colored paper on which he carried out this subtle masterpiece. In Flanders, in the fifteenth century, in the period from Van Eyck to Memling, we find that *silver point*, the most common of the metal points used for drawing, was the favorite tool.

In the fascinating, instructive detail, from an early

copy of a painting by the famous Fleming, Rogier van der Weyden, we see *St. Luke* (Plate 4), the patron saint of artists, actually at work with a *silver point*, drawing the head of the Virgin.

Pen and ink was a mode widely used by the old masters. The sharp point of pen or quill results in precise clarity, as in the crisp and moving sixteenth century masterpiece by Albrecht Dürer (Plate 33). Subtle gradations are rarely feasible with pen alone and when such gradations are desired, the artist tends to supplement his line with brush-strokes of the same color, illustrated with dazzling clarity by the last of the notable Venetian artists, the eighteenth century decorator of ceilings, G. B. Tiepolo (Plate 29). Another variation in pen drawing, illustrating the power that can be achieved by this mode, we observe in the timeless work of Rembrandt (Plate 46), where the greatest draughtsman of seventeenth century Holland fuses reality and a mood, with subtlety and force.

Drawings with *charcoal, black and red chalk*, and *pencil* offer an impressive variety of work, since with these, sharpness and delicate gradations of tone can be achieved. After the fifteenth century, when artists like Michelangelo (Plate 20) developed bolder effects of expression, attitude and gesture, they turned to black and red chalk, for with these they were able to present their ideas more broadly than had their predecessors with the metal point.

In the seventeenth century, in Flanders, Peter Paul Rubens (Plate 43) made some of his most significant drawings in red or black chalk or in a combination of both. Influenced by the eminent example of Rubens,

Watteau (see front cover), the foremost artist and draughtsman of the eighteenth century in France, carried on the same lovely tradition in countless studies, achieving a delicate amalgam of vivacity and sensitiveness. Our contemporary artists use pencil for rapid notation and for sketching, but only rarely do they use the hard chalk with which Raphael, Michelangelo, Holbein, Rubens and Watteau enchant us.

Since with *Pastel* an artist is enabled to employ a full range of colors it is perhaps stretching a point to include it here among the processes of drawing rather than of painting. Pastel is included, however, because *Portrait of Juvenal des Ursins* (Plate 49) is one of the earliest known pastels, done in 1455 by Fouquet, and also because it is akin to soft chalk. In the eighteenth century distinguished works in pastel were always classed as drawings. Starting with the French Impressionists, in the nineteenth century, both pastel and charcoal came to be favored materials.

With this much by way of background, we should be ready now, in the following chapters, to consider in further detail* the Great Drawings selected for this book.

---

*Limitations of space make an adequate exposition of the various ways in which drawings are made, the various pigments and tools employed, and a full account of the terms used in describing the materials of drawings, quite impossible. The serious student is, therefore, urged to consult the two authoritative books in English listed in the Recommended Reading:—(1) A. E. Popham's Handbook and (2) the Short Encyclopedia by Gettens and Stout.

II

ITALY

IN THE PAGES THAT FOLLOW, THE TERMS "Middle Ages" and "Mediaeval Art" refer to the period from the official recognition of Christianity—that is, the time of the Emperor Constantine (324-337 A.D.)—to about 1400, the beginning of the Renaissance in Italy. The Renaissance, as we shall see in due course, does not appear in Germany until considerably later.

The term "Romanesque" is not used in describing drawings, because on the whole, the use of that word had best be limited to a description of architecture, sculpture, and illuminated manuscripts. We do, however, speak of "Gothic" art which grew out of the Romanesque style in the twelfth century. Gothic is a proper designation, prior to the Renaissance, for all manifestations in the arts, whether in cathedrals and their adornment, domestic architecture, sculpture, tapestry weaving, manuscript illumination or drawing. The break with the Gothic tradition came in the fifteenth century in Italy.

The term "Renaissance" does not mean "rebirth"—but rather a renewed interest in antiquity, in learning and in science. Professor Chandler R. Post of Harvard

University has, more clearly than most scholars, described the diversity between the two ages, Gothic and Renaissance. "The latter," he says, "manifested itself in two principal channels:—in humanism, the more eager and intelligent comprehension of antiquity, and in individualism, the greater emphasis upon personality . . . The spirit of the age was revealed in art by the effort after a more truthful representation of actuality . . . One of the most interesting manifestations of the phenomenon was the evolution of universally talented geniuses such as Alberti, Leonardo da Vinci, and Michelangelo, who sought to realize to the fullest every possibility of man's personality. If humanism was the motive principle, individualism was the motive power of the Italian Renaissance. Helped by a passionate longing to vie with the ancients, it supplied the force for a period which, in artistic and intellectual achievement of every sort, can be paralleled only by the Periclean age . . . The whole Italian people had become a nation united, if not politically, at least by the craving for the beautiful in everything."

Let us now proceed and see how splendidly all this is reflected in some of the great drawings of the Renaissance in Europe.

PISANELLO

C. 1395 • 1455

We start our consideration of examples by supreme draughtsmen of the Italian Renaissance with *Two Studies of a Horse* (Plate 5) by Antonio Pisanello, whose activity in the service of princes was not confined to North Italy, the region of his birth. His few surviving, delicate, courtly paintings, with their profusion of flowers, animals and elegantly dressed figures, lack the compact, solid compositional qualities of his far-famed Florentine contemporaries:—Masaccio and Fra Angelico. His paintings betray his proximity to Teutonic lands. Pisanello is one of the most enchanting painters of the first half of the fifteenth century. We are, however, concerned here with the charm of his rich sketch books, as well as with the high significance of his world famous medals marked by classic restraint. These were factors of importance in the creation of the Renaissance style, in contrast with his paintings which hark back to the earlier Gothic period with their festive, delightful, realistic details.

In his drawings, as in his medals, an expressive outline is constant, combined with beauty of surface. Characteristic of the charm and sensitiveness of almost all of Pisanello's drawings of animals is the fact that the strikingly velvety surface and texture as well as the contours are realized through parallel shading with a multitude of fine lines, which do not detract from the essential form. Indeed the form, the structure, is actually supported by this characteristic surface treatment. Pisanello's drawings of horses emphasize his naturalistic curiosity. In our drawing we see his skill and veracity in the rendering of animals. The curious slitting of the nostrils of horses, shown in this and in other drawings by Pisanello, was apparently practised in earlier days by the Byzantines with the object of allowing their horses to breathe more freely. The practice is still prevalent among certain Mongol tribes. Such precise drawings of animals foreshadow the work of Leonardo.

POLLAIUOLO

c. 1432 • 1498

It may seem strange that such world famous artists as Masolino, Donatello, Masaccio, Brunelleschi, Uccello or Castagno, the founders of fifteenth century Florentine art, are omitted in a selection even as restricted as this. The fact is that no authentic drawings of the first three have survived and only four or five by Uccello. Indeed, few drawings of the early fifteenth century in Florence have come down to us. Hence any one of the twelve surviving drawings by Antonio Pollaiuolo, the most powerful and gifted of the Florentine naturalists, is of importance. Most of them illustrate his preoccupation with problems of anatomy and with the representation of the nude.

Antonio, the elder and by far the more gifted of the two artist sons of Jacopo Pollaiuolo (or the poulterer), was born in Florence, in 1432, if his father's declaration be correct. Legend says that he was apprenticed early with Bartoluccio di Michele, to learn the trade of the goldsmith. Like many another artist of that talented and versatile age, he was a master in many crafts besides the one in which he served his apprenticeship. A pupil of Castagno in painting, he was strongly original and amazingly powerful both on panel and in fresco painting. A pupil of Donatello in sculpture, he developed a rare command over bronze. Like Verrocchio, he was important both as a sculptor and as a painter. He was, also, a skilled designer in embroidery and an incomparable engraver.

Yet, master as he was in all these arts, it was as draughtsman that he stood out among his fellow artists, and it has been as draughtsman that he has since commanded the constant admiration of those who have known his work. Vasari speaks of his drawing continuously. In a short time he came to be considered the leader in the art of making designs. Cellini tells us that he was so great a draughtsman that nearly all the goldsmiths made use of his beautiful designs which were of so great an excellence that many sculptors and painters used them and thereby gained the greatest honor. The truth of Cellini's statement is borne out by countless examples. Even Raphael himself did not hesitate to borrow figures from Pollaiuolo. Thus his influence over the art of his time became as incalculable as it was far-reaching. During the second half of the fifteenth century he was the artist most interested in the study that more than any other marked the Florentine:—the study of the human figure. It is in him that we find concentrated that searchingly scientific and powerfully masculine spirit which makes him the connecting link between the commanding masters of form of the early fifteenth century—Uccello, Castagno and Donatello—and the giants of the coming age—Leonardo and Michelangelo.

Few of Pollaiuolo's highly prized drawings have survived. The number has been further reduced by present day criticism which, from the group once attributed to him, credits to the master's own hand scarcely more than a dozen drawings. One of these, the *Fighting Nudes*, of about 1460-1465, is now much discussed and with needless passion. For that reason, in spite of the temptation to reproduce the drawing, it is not included. It was the first rare and significant fifteenth century Italian drawing added, with delight and conviction, to the Fogg Museum collection almost forty years ago. Some of my keen-eyed juniors have used harsh words about it, but the majority of experienced connoisseurs continue to have faith in it, even though we admit that its quality has been impaired by restoration, like many an authentic painting or sculpture. This little story is told because only drawings about which there is complete agreement will be found in this book and because the incident illustrates Berenson's wise and well-known remark:—"Yet, when all is said and done, the ultimate appeal is to our feeling. From that responsibility no mechanical test, no material consideration, no peering in looking glasses, magical or not, can save us." Of the few pure drawings by Pollaiuolo, of undoubted authenticity, none is more famous than the *Adam* (Plate 6). The superb quality of the supple modelling places it among the great drawings of the Western World.

Observe in this outline type of Florentine drawing, in pen and brown wash, of Adam leaning on his hoe, produced with such economy of means, those qualities that are almost constant in Pollaiuolo's work:—a wiry, functional line, full of energy, which defines the form and suggests muscular effort. The modelling, you will note, is brought out by a discreet use of wash. It represents the kind of outline drawing which inspired

Botticelli. There are here also many of the national characteristics of style of the best of Italian Renaissance drawings:—a sculptural conception of form and the subordination of details in the interest of the harmonious rhythm of the whole design.

In his analysis of the expression of three-dimensional form, Professor Arthur Pope of Harvard says:—"Many superb examples of the use of line to express solid form are to be found among the drawings by the great masters of the Renaissance. . . ." In Pollaiuolo's *Adam* (Plate 6) we have ". . . an amazingly convincing rendering of solid form."

In speaking about the Adam and about the companion drawing of Eve, Berenson says:—". . . the line caresses as it models, makes you follow with keen pleasure every enveloping curve, every boss, every turn, makes you realize with the vividness of positive contact the texture of the skin, the elasticity of the flesh and the resistance of the muscles." Such words help us to *see*.

SIGNORELLI

c. 1441? • 1523

Luca Signorelli, born in Cortona, was a pupil of the great painter, Piero della Francesca, and reached maturity under Pollaiuolo at Florence. Note at once in the black chalk drawing of a *Nude Man and Kneeling Nude Woman* (Plate 7) that his figures are more heroic and robust than those of Pollaiuolo; also, that they are more animated in movement. Signorelli is a transitional artist who in his masterly chalk drawings revealed his genius. He was the first artist in Italy to exploit the use of black chalk. In all such studies Signorelli gives us ample proof that he was one of the early masters to use the nude as a vehicle of expression, increasing the solidity of the forms through his skillful use of shading.

In commenting on a similar drawing, also a study for the Cathedral of Orvieto frescoes, Berenson says:—"... And we, too, follow with pleasure these strokes that outline and model, light up, unite and harmonize. Few sketches have produced a more completely plastic-pictorial effect." He adds:—"Our artist was perhaps the only one who as a draughtsman travelled on his own legs the whole long way from Pollaiuolo (Plate 6) and the crystalline naturalism of the mid-quattrocento [the Italian term which means the 'four hundreds'] to the heroic proportions of Michelangelo (Plate 20), the almost too poignant accents of Andrea del Sarto, and the supple rhythms (Plate 27) of Tintoretto."

Signorelli blazes the way for the achievements of the High Renaissance and particularly for the powerful work of Michelangelo.

BOTTICELLI

1444? · 1510

ABUNDANCE

British Museum, London

Plate 9

MANTEGNA

1431 · 1506

JUDITH WITH THE HEAD OF HOLOFERNES

Uffizi, Florence

Plate 10

BONSIGNORI

c.1453 · 1519

PORTRAIT OF A VENETIAN SENATOR

Albertina, Vienna

Plate 11

ANTONELLO DA MESSINA

c.1430 · 1479?

PORTRAIT OF A BOY

Albertina, Vienna

Plate 12

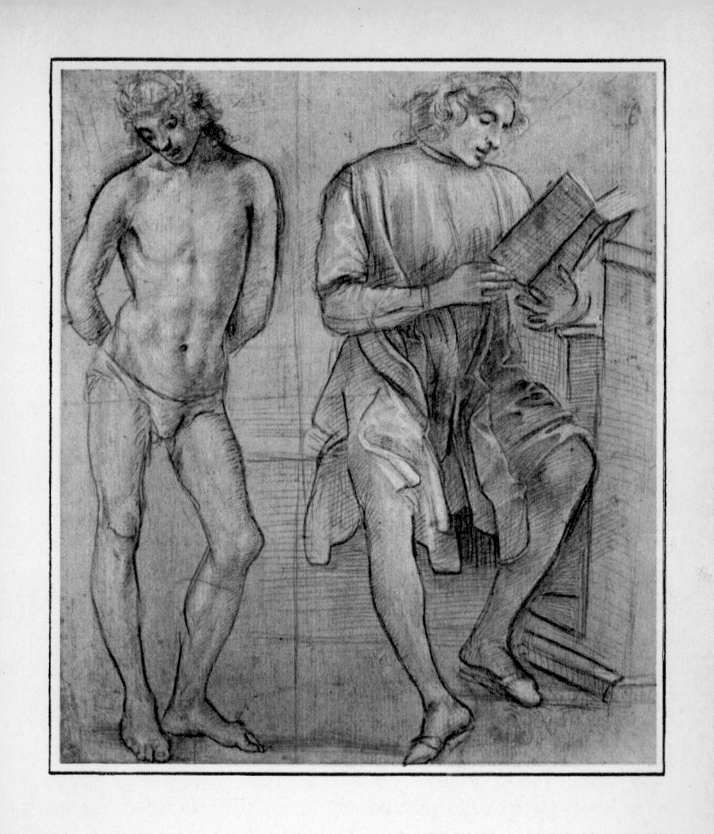

FILIPPINO LIPPI

c.1457 · 1504

STUDIES FOR A ST. SEBASTIAN AND A SEATED FIGURE

Metropolitan Museum of Art, New York

Plate 13

Plate 14

LEONARDO

1452 · 1519

STUDY FOR A HORSE AND RIDER

John Nicholas Brown, Providence

LEONARDO

1452 · 1519

STUDIES OF HANDS

Royal Library, Windsor

Plate 15

LEONARDO

1452 · 1519

HEAD OF A YOUNG WOMAN

Royal Library, Windsor

LEONARDO

1452 · 1519

SELF PORTRAIT

Royal Library, Turin

Plate 17

MICHELANGELO

1475 · 1564

STUDIES FOR THE LIBYAN SIBYL

Metropolitan Museum of Art, New York

Plate 18

MICHELANGELO

1475 · 1564

CHRIST'S RESURRECTION

British Museum, London

Plate 19

MICHELANGELO

1475 · 1564

HEAD OF A LOST SOUL

Royal Library, Windsor

PERUGINO

1446 · 1523

FOUR STANDING APOSTLES

Fogg Museum of Art, Harvard University

Plate 21

RAPHAEL

1483 · 1520

SELF PORTRAIT

Ashmolean Museum, Oxford

Plate 22

RAPHAEL

1483 · 1520

ST. GEORGE AND THE DRAGON

Uffizi, Florence

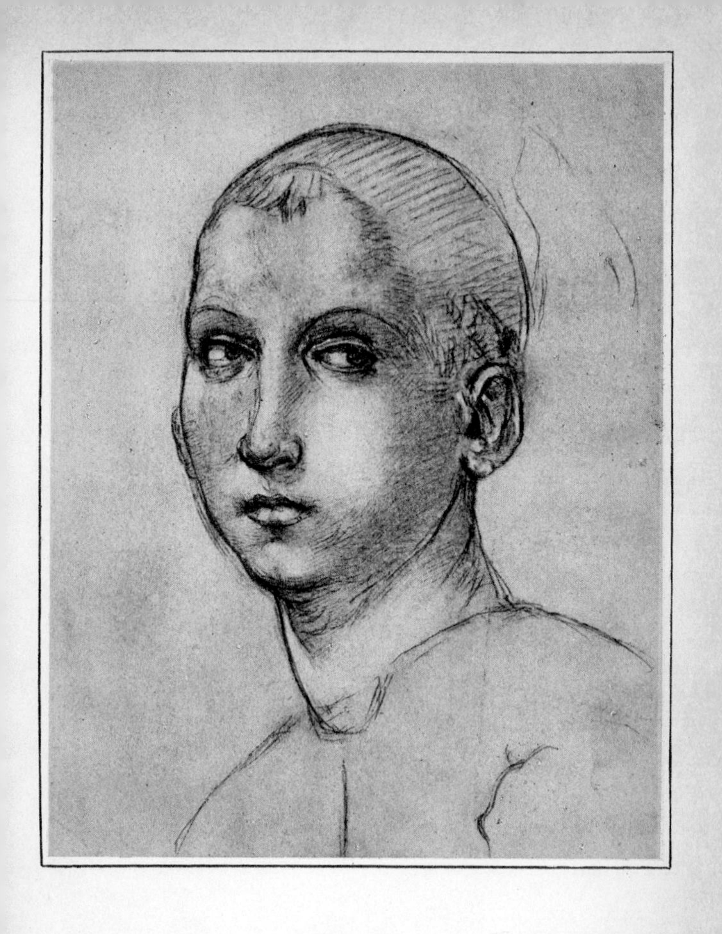

RAPHAEL

1483 · 1520

STUDY OF ST. PLACIDUS *(detail)*

Ashmolean Museum, Oxford

Plate 24

RAPHAEL

1483 · 1520

MADONNA WITH POMEGRANATE

Albertina, Vienna

Plate 25

VERROCCHIO

1435 • 1488

Andrea del Verrocchio, an eminent teacher, with manifold and varied interests which included anatomy, music, mathematics and perspective, is best known, perhaps, as the last great sculptor of the Early Renaissance in Italy. He has to his credit one of the most satisfactory of all equestrian statues, the statue to the military leader, Colleoni, in Venice. What is less well known is his profound influence on his followers:—on Perugino, Lorenzo di Credi and most of all on his greatest pupil, Leonardo, who, while he derived from his master types and motifs, soared far above him in genius.

The life-sized, monumental, spirited drawing of the *Head of a Woman* (Plate 8) lacks Pollaiuolo's violence. It is one of the boldest and most inspiring masterpieces of fifteenth century draughtsmanship. This beautiful drawing, one of the glories of the superb collection at Christ Church, Oxford, is today, by general consent, given to Verrocchio. We find in it a sculptural conception of form; great stability; an engaging mood and real clarity of structure. There is about this calm drawing a rare combination of grace and solidity.

BOTTICELLI

1444? • 1510

Masaccio, Uccello, Domenico Veneziano and Fra Filippo Lippi were the four outstanding artists of the first half of the fifteenth century who deeply influenced Florentine painting. As there are few drawings by them that have come down to us, we pass at once to the very personal art of Sandro Botticelli, the most distinguished pupil of Fra Filippo Lippi, to consider his exquisite, poetic drawing of *Abundance* (Plate 9), long looked upon as perhaps the most beautiful Florentine drawing in the world. It is not a study for a painting, but a drawing done for its own sake and highly finished. It is a supreme, faultless masterpiece, strongly reminiscent of his lyrical paintings:—*The Allegory of Spring* and *The Birth of Venus*, both commissioned by Lorenzo de' Medici.

The allegorical figure of Abundance, a treasure of the British Museum, London, is a fine pen drawing with brown wash on a light reddish ground heightened with white, done immediately after Botticelli's return from Rome in 1482. The horn of plenty and the children on the left are done in black chalk. Note particularly this mixed technique because it is original, sensitive, and refined in its subtle combination of graphic material, and because it illustrates the originality with which a true master is able to handle various media. While as a rule we speak of Botticelli as a linearist, it is clear that in this masterpiece there is added a tonal effect which is the result of a skillful combination in the use of brush and pen.

Berenson has described the drawing in words of haunting beauty:—"A great master of line, like Botticelli," he says, "does not need the help of the pencil to emphasize the revelation of his brush. The same touch of the whimsical, the same dreamy grace, the same subtlety of refinement, that we learned to love in his pictures, meet us once more in his sketches, and there is always present the line which envelops, models and realizes with such a vivacity and speed in communicating itself, that, if you do not frighten away its shy influence by too coldly testing the anatomical correctness of its creations, you quickly find yourself not looking at the form, but caressing it with your eyes, not contemplating, but living the action. After the Spring, and his Venus rising from the Sea, and on a level certainly, with his Villa Lemmi frescoes, the most beautiful and the most intimately characteristic of Sandro Botticelli's achievements is . . . (this drawing) a nymph, the Flora of the Spring, but grown older, with the high ecstasy of the months spent between sowing and in gathering, older, but none the less a maenad, with her hair streaming wildly to the wind, hastens joyously through the land, followed by a train of roguish children. The soft meshes of her lambent draperies cling to her slender, firm-fleshed figure, revealing her form as if it were nude, and conveying the action all the better for their fluttering away from the limbs, drawn in the opposite direction by the breeze. Her arm, it is true, is much longer than arms usually are, but here the composition required this length, and Sandro did not disdain to make it reach down from her shoulder to the hand of the little child who runs sportively beside her. You might easily find other faults in this sheet, if you chose, and would doubtless dwell upon them until its splendour disappeared; but in many of the world's great masterpieces it is wiser to discount at a glance such failings as all may discern and devote ourselves if we are able, to wooing the indwelling soul of the beauty."

Observe this drawing closely in order to see how the body appears to move with enchanting lightness as if wafted, in its translucent draperies, over the ground. A gentle breeze seems to envelop the figures and carry them forward.

MANTEGNA

1431 • 1506

Andrea Mantegna of Padua, the founder of humanistic painting in North Italy, spent much of his life in Mantua, on being called to be court painter of Federigo Gonzaga, Marquis of Mantua. He gave form to his austere and lofty conceptions with equal force in color, monochrome or with the graver. Handling with meticulous mastery the pen or fine brush, he achieved an unsurpassed plastic force and firmness which make his figures as strong and hard as cast bronze. Their draperies are both crisp and immovable. No other artist can equal his high seriousness or his direct, stern, contained and majestic grandeur. His influence on subsequent art was profound not only in Italy but north of the Alps as well. Dürer was his admirer and Rembrandt as late as the seventeenth century studied his engravings with real understanding. Charles I of England acquired a group of his paintings—*The Triumph of Caesar*—still extant in Hampton Court Palace.

The picture of *Judith with the Head of Holofernes* (Plate 10) is one of the limited group of authentic drawings by Mantegna, the commanding leader of the Paduan school, who in his youth was inspired by Donatello. It reveals his power as a draughtsman and the high quality of his work, which, in rendering form, combines linear charm with sculptural solidity. His inspiration was Greco-Roman art, not nature. Mantegna, in combining the style of Donatello with his own, influenced markedly Giovanni Bellini and the Venetians, as well as the later Florentines. There are copies of this splendid pen and ink drawing in the Louvre, at Munich and in the British Museum. Indeed, the subject was treated frequently by Mantegna and his followers. One of the most gem-like pictures in the Widener Bequest at the National Gallery, Washington is of this same subject.

Giorgio Vasari of Arezzo, a painter of the High Renaissance—an architect, a businessman, a devoted friend of Michelangelo, and a collector of drawings—is today valued primarily for his pleasantly written, gossipy but important series of artists' biographies, his famous *Lives of the Most Excellent Architects, Painters and Sculptors of Italy*, dedicated to Cosimo de' Medici. It is an invaluable and a fascinating source book for students of Italian art, even if we had better take much that he records with a grain of salt. In his biography of Mantegna, he refers, in all probability, to this very drawing when he says:—"There is in our portfolio . . . a drawing by Andrea of a Judith placing the head of Holofernes in a wallet held by a Negro slave. It is in black and white but the manner of handling the whites is no longer used. The artist left the white paper to serve for the high light. It is done with so much delicacy that hairs are distinguishable, and one might regard this as a painting [monochrome] rather than as a drawing."

We can trace in the work of *Francesco Bonsignori* (c. 1453-1519) (Plate 11) the strong influence of Mantegna in portraiture. This is a black chalk study for the signed picture of a *Venetian Senator*, dated 1487, in the National Gallery, London. With all its animated charm of eyes and mouth, with all its grand solidity, it lacks by a little the full impressiveness of a work by Mantegna, to be found, shall we say, in portraits of the Gonzagas at Mantua.

The superb, appealing, sculptural head of the *Portrait of a Boy* (Plate 12), at one time attributed to the School of Mantegna, at another time to Bellini, is in fact the only known drawing by *Antonello da Messina* (c. 1430-1497?), who, though he came from Sicily, and was educated in Naples by Colantonio, was one of the founders of Venetian portrait drawing, who instead of the North Italian device of profile drawing, presented the subject in three-quarters profile. Antonello da Messina had come to know the technique of oil of the school of Van Eyck and was one of the first to master that procedure. He was in Venice about 1475 and as an innovator of great influence introduced this more luminous and richer method and gave it wide currency. He and Mantegna were Bellini's most distinguished predecessors. Note in the drawing the masterly, vigorous, vital presentation; the forthright monumentality, the areas of light and dark that define the humanistic, geometric idea of form. It is in portraits of this realistic type, whether in painting or in drawing, that Antonello da Messina excels.

FILIPPINO LIPPI

c. 1457 • 1504

To round out our picture of the second half of the fifteenth century we ought to consider two very different contemporaries: – the undervalued, versatile, highstrung, sensitive Filippino Lippi and the calmer, less emotional anticipator of the monumental, classical style of the early sixteenth century, Ghirlandaio, teacher of Michelangelo. These two popular mural painters were more distinguished as draughtsmen than as painters. We illustrate, however, only Filippino Lippi, the son of Fra Filippo Lippi, and the pupil of Botticelli, in the studies for a *St. Sebastian and a Seated Figure Reading* (Plate 13), one of the treasures of the Metropolitan Museum of Art, New York. Like so many of the drawings by Filippino this is an exquisite silver point and brush drawing on a lovely pink prepared surface, heightened with white.

Agnes Mongan in her book on *One Hundred Master Drawings*, says:–"Filippino was a Florentine in his concentration on the human figure, but his was not the scientific interest of the masters of the earlier Quattrocento, such as Masaccio and Uccello, or their artistic descendants in the second half of the century, such as Pollaiuolo, Leonardo and Michelangelo. By nature he was a sensitive spirit, whose drawings have a rather pervasive melancholy but he was neither searching nor profound. The folds and movement of drapery engaged his attention as much as or sometimes more than the figures beneath. For that reason his direct studies from the model, such as these, are often fresher and more lively than the paintings made from them. He drew the nude rarely, seldom with the success he has achieved in this study for a Saint Sebastian . . . Looking at the finely outlined contours of the nude figure, and the play of light over the drapery of the other figure we can agree with Berenson that 'Filippino was no unworthy pupil of Botticelli and no despicable contemporary of Leonardo.'"

Filippino's position in Florence during his lifetime was a high one, and Vasari records that when he died a man still under fifty, he was mourned with honours usually granted only to princes. In addition to his talents as an artist, his always courteous, affable and gentle manner had won him a host of friends.

The testimony of his work bears out the testimony of his friends. It reveals a character neither robust nor tenacious, but tender, gracious with a love of both movement and calm, with real religious intensity, winning sentiment and gentle melancholy. In taste, he stands a little apart from his contemporaries of more powerful stature and more scientific interests but like them he was indefatigable in his interest in solving problems connected with his art. He filled page upon page with figure sketches drawn in silver point on prepared papers, of rose, violet, gray and beige, and in pen and ink on white paper. Benvenuto Cellini, who was for a time the inseparable companion of one of Filippino's sons, writes that "the house was still full of the beautiful studies made by his gifted father." Later he remarks:—"There were several books of drawings." Vasari in his life of Filippino boasts possession of one of these sketch books.

• • •

The early sixteenth century, the Cinquecento (the "five hundreds"), is the most notable period in Italian art and indeed, one of the most important in Europe, covering as it does the time of Leonardo da Vinci, Michelangelo, Raphael, Titian, as well as Dürer and Holbein in Germany.

It was a period of intense rivalry among rich and princely patrons. That was true also of the leading artists who consciously strove to broaden their outlook through scholarly and scientific as well as artistic pursuits, thus changing their age old status and moving from the world of mere craftsmanship to the commanding position of creative artists competed for and respected by these same princely patrons.

LEONARDO

1452 • 1519

The oldest of the renowned artists of the epoch—the deeply indebted and most gifted pupil of Verrocchio—

Leonardo da Vinci—was born in Tuscany, the illegitimate son of a successful notary and a peasant mother.

Vasari tells the familiar story of how Leonardo as a boy painted a dragon on the shield of one of his father's peasants: "And for this purpose carried into a room of his own, lizards great and small, crickets, serpents, butterflies, grasshoppers, bats and such like animals, out of which he formed a great ugly creature."

By 1469 Leonardo was living in Florence and in 1472 at the age of twenty, he had become a member of the guild of St. Luke, though still in Verrocchio's workshop as late as 1476. Problems of form and volume, of perspective, of the mass and movement of the human body, of balance and harmony, preoccupied Leonardo as they did all of the experimental Florentine artists and these preoccupations are revealed in their drawings.

Leonardo studied the anatomy of horses, worked out a theory of their proportions and drew them throughout his career with close observation as is clearly revealed in the *Horse and Rider* (Plate 14), an exquisite drawing from the collection of John Nicholas Brown, Providence, Rhode Island. It is a small early drawing of about 1480 done in silver point on a paper prepared with a light gray ground. "Surely," says Agnes Mongan, "no words could possibly give the effect of movement of this horse and rider coming forward with a powerful easy rhythm out of the background. With his acute instantaneous vision, Leonardo has seen the rider with his head up and with it lowered and has revealed both. If one 'reads' the drawing looking first at the rider as he looks to the left and then as he looks down, it adds to the sense of movement, using the same principle as moving picture film . . . In no other hand has the silver point been used to give such marvellously precise plastic forms or such a sense of surface texture. Leonardo, a lefthanded artist, almost inevitably shades, as here, from left to right."

The beautiful silver point *Studies of Hands* (Plate 15) at Windsor Castle may have been preparatory studies for one of his early portraits of 1474, now damaged. In this drawing, Leonardo makes us aware of the long jointed fingers. He does much more, however, than to tell us the mere facts about these hands for in this inspired drawing he emphasizes their beauty and does so through the delicate rendering of light and shade.

One of the most superb of Italian drawings with its faint suggestion of a quizzical smile is a study from life for the *Head of a Young Woman* (Plate 16),* in the *Virgin of the Rocks* in the Louvre, a commission which Leonardo received in 1483. It is not an overstatement to speak of the drawing as one of the most beautiful in the world, in which Leonardo aims at the fullest plastic statement and in which Sir Kenneth Clark notes that the balance between natural and ideal beauty is perfectly held. Berenson asks us to observe the quality of the contours, the exquisite firmness of the modelling, the enigmatic beauty of the conception and the apparent effortlessness of the execution.

Here we see also Leonardo's leadership in a certain classic tendency coupled with a marked mystic note. This mystic, enigmatic expression he realizes chiefly

*See footnote 1, page 108.

in the way he draws the corners of the mouth and the corners of the two totally different, strange eyes. It is these that give the haunting expression to the face.

The only authentic *Self Portrait* of Leonardo, in his last years (Plate 17), is done in a firm, clear style. Sir Kenneth Clark has characterized this red chalk self-portrait in the Royal Library, Turin, in part in these words:—". . . This great furrowed mountain of a face with its noble brow, commanding cavernous eyes and undulating foothills of beard is like the faces of all the great men of the nineteenth century as the camera has perceived them for us—Darwin, Tolstoi, Walt Whitman. Time, with its spectacle of human suffering, has reduced them all to a common level of venerability."

MICHELANGELO

1475 • 1564

Let us look now at three superb drawings (Plates 18, 19 and 20), by the titanic sculptor, the towering genius in painting, poetry and architecture—Michelangelo Buonarroti, who was a generation younger than Leonardo and outlived him by almost half a century. At the age of thirteen Michelangelo was apprenticed to the narrative painter Ghirlandaio, in whose workshop he was well grounded in all methods of painting and drawing. On that early foundation he built solidly through an intensive study of the works of earlier Florentine giants, reinforced by his deep devotion to and passionate, enthusiastic study of classical sculpture in the Medici Collection of antiques—supplemented and modified by his study of anatomy.

His thoughtful, passionate force of character was reflected in his work, with its love for contorted nudes to express emotion through the device of turning one part of the body in a different direction from another, and yet balancing the parts of the body, called *contrapposto*, in Italian. This and all other aspects of his grandiose production made a profound impression on his contemporaries, comparable only to that of his competitor and rival, the genius, Leonardo da Vinci.

Born in Tuscany, Michelangelo first reached Rome in 1496 and there spent much of his life, starting in 1505 in the service of Pope Julius II. In 1508, in his early thirties, he was already at work on the ceiling of the famous Sistine Chapel—so-called because it had been built by Pope Sixtus IV. For the decoration of this ceiling, an achievement of unbelievable power and grandeur, and full of deepest human content, he revealed magnificently the Renaissance ideal of heroic beauty, through the skillful use of the human body in every conceivable posture. For that ceiling he studied and worked out all the details in careful drawings of high significance, and in them are revealed his power as a sculptor, as a draughtsman and above all as a commanding personality.

Michelangelo looked upon his drawings not as an end in themselves, but as necessary study material, as first steps, as means to an end. They are, however particularly fascinating because in them we feel the impact of his creative, his deeply human spirit.

Since you may have the opportunity to look at the

exciting original drawing at the Metropolitan Museum, New York, we select the convincing study for the *Libyan Sibyl* (Plate 18) for the ceiling of the Sistine Chapel. This sheet of studies was well described by Bryson Burroughs, a gifted painter and the Curator of Paintings, at the time that the drawing entered the Metropolitan Museum collection. It will increase our powers of observation to follow, with patience, the details of the drawing as he does. Among other things he says that it is:—". . . a superb, carefully finished nude study in red chalk for the upper part of the body of the Sibyl, drawn from a masculine figure. The chalk lines . . . model with great force the forms of the head and the mighty back and arms . . . Great care has been given to the anatomical structure of the figure, and the muscles show with more distinctness and salience than they would even in the most highly trained athlete . . . The figure has been thought of 'in the round,' from all sides, as a sculptor would conceive it, and not as an appearance of the model from one position only, the usual practice of painters. The structure and forms, directly suggested by the actual figure in front of him, were the artist's preoccupation in the making of this sketch. Nothing would have been gained by drawing the hair of this model in a study which was to serve for a female figure, and so the hair is slurred over. The hands, though convincing in mass and action, lack distinctness in details of form. A large scale drawing of the left hand with attention to these particulars occupies the lower center of the sheet. Alongside of it is a second study of the face, drawn with great delicacy, which approaches in expression the face of the

Sibyl in the fresco. Above the head and impinging upon it, the left side of the torso has again been sketched in loose, rapid lines with a more upright action than in the finished drawing and with the arm in more violent perspective. On the lower right of the page are three large-scale studies having to do with the left foot. It is shown completely with the ankle in one drawing and the great toe alone in the third, each sketch differing from the others in the degree of the push of the toes against the floor."

Berenson describes the black chalk drawing of *Christ's Resurrection* (Plate 19), in the British Museum, in part, in these words:—"The most carefully thought-out and noblest of designs for this subject. Here Christ floats away as in a dream, like a rising mist, and even the soldiers have less agitated attitudes. The greatest merit of this composition is, perhaps, its spaciousness; and the pictorial intention is, for Michelangelo, singularly clear."

The black chalk drawing of the *Head of a Lost Soul* (Plate 20), Royal Library, Windsor, roaring with rage or pain and reminiscent in feeling of Leonardo da Vinci, was made about twenty-two years after the Libyan Sibyl. In concentrating on this drawing we realize that verbal description can not possibly do justice to this raging, roaring, tortured dynamic head, which though not identical with any particular head in the famous fresco, is nonetheless connected with the overpowering grandeur of the Last Judgment in the Sistine Chapel. There is here revealed the majesty of the Renaissance combined with an unforgettable tragic note.

In concluding our brief consideration of only three of Michelangelo's characteristic drawings let us remember that he was the most important sculptor of Europe in the sixteenth century. Post says of him:— "His influence was paramount during the epoch and has continued to be a vital factor in art down to our own day . . . He was, by nature, essentially a sculptor and he conceived and executed his paintings (and drawings) from the sculptor's standpoint . . . Though he derived his love of the nude from the antique, he did not acquire his anatomy from Greek and Roman figures but from life . . . His own personality was so powerful that it permeated all his productions and saved them from the prevalent danger of vacuity . . . The most vital influences that played upon him were the writings of Dante and the personality of Savonarola."

PERUGINO

1446 • 1523

"Perugino, during his later years, was one of the most documented of Renaissance artists, but there are only tradition and the explanation which the work itself offers, to tell of his early training. Vasari says that he worked with Luca Signorelli under Piero della Francesca at Arezzo. In 1472 he was in Florence, where he was enrolled in the Guild of the Painters, and where, it is said, Verrocchio was his master. It was not long before his work was winning wondering admiration and praise. His fame spread with phenomenal quickness. Orders poured in upon him, and we find him hurrying from place to place to execute them. In the same year he is recorded at work in Perugia, Orvieto, Rome and Florence. Other documents speak of his work in Lucca, Siena and Bologna. Orvieto begged him to return from Rome, where he had gone on a summons from the Pope to paint in the Sistine Chapel. Venice sent for him. The Duke of Milan wrote to his ambassadors telling them to use their influence to entice him to Milan. Isabella Gonzaga dispatched beseeching letters over a span of years, trying to make the unwilling artist paint an allegorical picture for the famous series in her study. We wonder now at such sudden deep enthusiasm. At that time, however, his infinitely peaceful landscapes, peopled by saints cut off from everything but the contemplation of their own visions, were strikingly new. It is recorded that the people in Perugia ran to see his paintings. His fresco in the Sistine Chapel, *Christ Giving the Keys to St. Peter*, was epochal in its new order and symmetry, its noble sweep of distance, its calm and grandeur. In such light and air and order, however, the figures soon came to be of secondary importance. Since he was by nature uninterested in variety and was always pressed for orders, Perugino at the turn of the century took the easier way—that of repetition. The same figures, and even the same compositions, he and his assistants used again and again. His never-changing rhythms became monotonous, the pretty faces insipid, the undulating hills and feathery trees tedious. One hoped for a stirring of the air or a sudden vigorous movement, but it never came. Criticism began to replace praise, criticism that became a storm of censure. Michelangelo openly called Perugino a dolt. Florence, where he had planned to live out his last days, became hostile. In a few brief years his most gifted pupil, Raphael, won a name that surpassed Perugino's at its height.

Selling his possessions in Florence, he returned to provincial Perugia, where his fame waned with his years. Old, scorned, and almost forgotten, he died of the plague in 1523.

Perugino at the height of his powers kept a bustling shop of assistants. Some of the latter proved such proficient draughtsmen that their drawings occasionally pass today as Perugino, but the difference is striking between the copies and variations of assistants and Perugino's own draughtsmanship. Note in the brush drawing of *Four Standing Apostles* (Plate 21)—a study for the large altarpiece of the Ascension, in the Lyons Museum—that his line is pliant and sensitive, his touch light, sure and easy, his contours firm but delicate, his shading in quick decisive strokes. The hands and feet have a tense liveliness, as though caught in a second of suspended action. The eyes and mouths, even in the slightest sketches, have the same sense of introspection and contemplation as have the paintings. The majority of the drawings done before 1500 were produced in silver point. Until recently this drawing has been called silver point, but in its purest passages it is a brush drawing." *

*Fogg Museum of Art. *Drawings by Agnes Mongan and Paul J. Sachs.* Harvard University Press, 1946. 3v. (Text and plates.)

RAPHAEL

1483 • 1520

Raphael's place among the greatest of European draughtsmen is secure. His drawings of exquisite feeling have always been valued by connoisseurs. He has been one of the very few to survive reversals of taste and changes of fashion, remaining from his day until our own one of the best known and most loved of artists. A precocious youth, he more than fulfilled his early radiant promise. He learned readily, absorbed quickly, and developed rapidly his own personal style. His drawings, whether of his provincial Umbrian youth, his Florentine period, when he first knew the work of Leonardo and Michelangelo, or the last Roman years, when he became one of the glories and ornaments of the full Renaissance, are all marked by a rounded incomparable grace more often subtly suggested than described, rhythms which have a measured swing even in violent action, and a dominating pervasive sentiment, as refined and delicate as it is strong. In short, we find in his appealing work a perfect combination of Florentine knowledge, Umbrian sweetness, and his own engaging personal ideal of beauty, already revealed, as early as 1499, in his gracious, boyish *Self Portrait* (Plate 22), a treasure of the Ashmolean Museum, which houses so many of the master's finest drawings.

Pope Julius II (1503-1513) and Pope Leo X (1513-

1521) were the powerful patrons of Raphael. As court painter of Pope Julius II, and art dictator of Rome, Raphael decorated the most famous of the apartments in the Vatican—"The Stanze"—just as Michelangelo had been entrusted with the decoration of the ceiling of the Sistine Chapel. About that time Leonardo arrived in Rome so that for a limited period the three giants of the Renaissance were in Rome together.

In his work in the Vatican as in this early *Self Portrait* and in every other picture and drawing, we are made aware of Raphael's search for perfection; his ideal of beauty; his well-trained hand always at the command of his astonishingly keen eye.

One of his masterly drawings representing a scene of action is the pen and brown ink drawing done about 1500-1502, of *St. George and the Dragon* (Plate 23), a cartoon for the painting in the Louvre in which the beauty and grace of the finished picture already permeate this rapid sketch. Another version of the same subject is treated in one of the most wonderful and most perfectly preserved of Raphael's paintings, now in the National Gallery, Washington.

In spite of the apparent ease and dash of the silver point drawing from Oxford, a study for the head of *S. Placidus* (Plate 24) in a fresco of the Trinity and Saints in Perugia, there is evident, as always, clarity and harmony.

"No mediaeval draughtsman," says Middeldorf, "could have been more scrupulous in his work. And yet none of Raphael's pictures have become pedestrian through the lengthy efforts spent on them. To the last, Raphael kept alive the fire of his first inspiration. He fed it with hard toil. Therefore his drawings are as much a part of his accomplishment as his pictures."

In the chalk drawing of the *Madonna with Pomegranate* (Plate 25), of about 1504, from the Albertina, Vienna, we find fully realized the ideal of the Madonna of the Renaissance. It is one of the finest drawings of one of the loveliest Madonnas by Raphael. We are captivated by the perfect rhythms, the serenity and the unity of this masterpiece, as our eyes travel from the head of the Madonna to the Pomegranate held by both Mother and Child, and then to the book.

It is helpful to compare drawings in order to appreciate more fully the qualities of the particular work under consideration. Looking back (Plate 9) at Botticelli's *Abundance*, what are the contrasts that strike us in comparing that drawing with this one? In the Botticelli, observe a fusion of the real and the ideal, with the emphasis on the ideal—a subtle other-world spiritual quality. In the Raphael (Plate 25), in spite of tenderness, we are more aware of the weight and structure of the figures. In short, in the Raphael there is a balanced combination of physical and spiritual beauty. Also characteristic of the style of Italian Renaissance drawings in the Raphael is the clear, firm, sculptural conception of form; the significance of the contours and the sensitive subordination of details in the interest of the over-all design. It will be helpful, at this point also, to contrast Raphael's Madonna and Child with a characteristic drawing of the same subject by Schongauer (Plate 30), in which the form, you will note, is part and parcel of the garment; in which the ornamental lines emphasize details rather than the sculptural character of the figures. In short, as in all the more calligraphic work of Northern artists, we feel in the Schongauer that the decorative line is an end in itself. That certainly is not true of the Raphael.

Middeldorf's comment will help us still further:—"It is a commonplace to refer to Raphael's madonnas as the perfect representation of Mother and Child. But it is worthwhile to examine them carefully one by one to discover how many variations Raphael could develop from the traditional theme. The means which he employed were not new. Every conceit that he used seems to have been coined in the preceding century; his Virgins recall those of Donatello, Desiderio da Settignano, Rossellino and the other Florentines. Leonardo and Michelangelo inspired him. And yet the spirit of his Virgins is new; though grown in dignity, they are more human than those of the older masters, they are not as precious as Desiderio's madonnas; they do not have the sadness of those by Donatello and Michelangelo. And Leonardo attained only in a few drawings the easy grace which distinguished every single one of Raphael's madonnas . . . *beauty*, *truth*, *expression* . . . receive their peculiar quality through his grace: his beauty never chills or overawes; his truth is never injudicious or indiscreet, his expression never forced or strained. Everything is at its perfect ease."

wash; the chalk studies of heads or figures; and the highly finished pen and wash drawings heightened with white on colored blue-green paper. Of these the *Rest on the Flight into Egypt* (Plate 28) resembles in effect the chiaroscuro woodcuts so popular in the second half of the sixteenth century. Few drawings of this highly finished type from Veronese's hands survive.

Many of his fascinating, rapid pen sketches have come to light in recent years. In them there is no suggestion, as here, of the rich materials and trappings of Veronese's paintings, in which the Virgin is represented as an aristocrat.

TIEPOLO

1696 • 1770

While it is in France that we reach the heights of eighteenth century gaiety, it is to Italy and more particularly to Venice and to the work of Gian Battista Tiepolo, the artistic descendant of the Venetians of the Renaissance, that we must look for the inspiration that the Rococo artists of France found in his brilliant performances.

Tiepolo was the last of the inspired Venetian decorators of vast ceilings and wall surfaces. He can be well seen at Würzburg, at the Carmine in Venice and at the Royal Palace in Madrid. In all of his prolific work we delight in the illusion of Italian sunlight which suffused his rapid sketches as it does his vast compositions. The best prints and drawings by Tiepolo are the glistening performances of an artist, who was the darling of a sophisticated and mature society that was about to vanish. In their inimitable, luminous drawings Tiepolo and his contemporaries—Guardi, Canaletto and Piranesi—helped directly and indirectly to mould art in France in the eighteenth century.

With Tiepolo's passing went not only the most prolific, scintillating and lighthearted of decorative painters, but the last notable Venetian painter in the great tradition. From youth to age his fancy did not falter nor his energy fail. Throughout a long life his brush remained at the command of a vivid and inexhaustible imagination. He seems to have drawn as easily as he breathed, and his drawings, whether preliminary studies for altarpieces and ceilings, or sketches dashed off for his own pure pleasure, are all placed on the page with a faultless knowledge of space, proportion and foreshortening. The light beloved of all Venetians shines on his pages with a brilliant whiteness. Note in the typical pen and brown wash drawing of *The Rest on the Flight into Egypt* (Plate 29) how through the magic of his technique the untouched highlights seem brighter than reality. A swift pen line of curves and flourishes delineates the fleeting contours. A single warm transparent wash with sharp, dark accents makes the shadows, from which the figures emerge into a dazzling light which drowns all small details and seems to absorb the very shadows themselves. Only Rembrandt at an earlier day produced drawings, though more moving and profound, in which light and dark played with such force.

III

GERMANY

IN GERMANY, AS IN OTHER COUNTRIES north of the Alps, the Renaissance came later than in Italy, because during most of the fifteenth century artists continued to be swayed by the vitality of the Gothic spirit. With but few exceptions the true significance, the true distinction of the work of German artists, internationally viewed, is to be found not in their paintings but in their engravings, woodcuts and drawings. In every graphic medium they are supreme for almost a hundred years—that is during the late fifteenth century and for about the first half of the sixteenth century. After that the decline of German art may be explained by the disasters of the Thirty Years' War, which prevented any significant development in the field of art for a hundred years. In other European lands, during the fifteenth and sixteenth centuries the graphic arts were far less practised for their own sake as vehicles for the expression of ideas and for the creation of visual images that could, on fragile pieces of paper, be spread far and wide. Schongauer's prints, for instance, travelled as far afield as

Italy and Spain and in those countries influenced painters and sculptors. Even Raphael was inspired by them and Michelangelo was impressed by Schongauer's engraving of the *Temptation of St. Anthony*. Trained as engravers or metalworkers, the drawings of German artists are characterized by sharpness and clarity of accent. South of the Alps when painters turned to engraving and drawing we find, by contrast, breadth and harmony rather than the emotional, decorative works of the North.

In Italy and in Flanders drawings were, as a rule, first steps or studies, produced not as aesthetic and decorative ends in themselves but rather as preparations for fresco or panel paintings. In Germany engravings, woodcuts and drawings were often produced as quite independent works of art. This does not mean that German art was uninfluenced by Italian or more especially by Flemish art. In spite of those influences, which at times were very marked, as we shall see, giants like Dürer and Holbein never sacrificed the native flavor of their work.

It has often been suggested that as in music so in the graphic arts the emotional quality in German work is to be accounted for by the fundamental character of Teutonic imagination. This emotional impulse, this lack of restraint, is not only inherent in the content of their works but also in the free play of the expressive, decorative, ornamental lines employed by them.

The Germans drew inspiration from their romantic love of nature, in its detailed as well as in its larger aspects. Inherent also in their art is a homely, emotional religious feeling.

Let us now look at a few specific examples to illustrate the general observations just made.

SCHONGAUER

c. 1445 • 1491

Martin Schongauer was the most captivating of the German artists active in the last quarter of the fifteenth century, in whose work technical skill, logical clarity and harmony are notable. He based his procedure on Flemish precedent without, however, a sacrifice of his national characteristics. He is peculiarly Gothic in his graceful language of form. The lovely, dignified *Virgin and Child* (Plate 30), like all of his superb prints, offers proof that his early training was received in a goldsmith's workshop. It is finished with meticulous care. It is not only one of the finest black and white works by Schongauer but also a splendid example of early Northern art; a mature work by a Gothic genius. It is one of the most appealing, most wonderfully delineated of all of Schongauer's madonnas, touched by something of the Flemish nobility inherent in the work of Rogier van der Weyden, but with indigenous German modifications. Many of the early Gothic elements are still in evidence:—the angular, slender, pointed fingers which bring out the expressive character of the hands; the sharp angular folds of opulent, agitated drapery of exaggerated elegance and abstract decorative pattern, which serve as a vehicle of expression. All this is produced with crisp accents and fine gradations of pen and ink from black to gray:—the ever present ornamental play of lines.

MASTER OF THE HOUSE BOOK

(Last quarter of the Fifteenth Century)

The Master of the House Book, is so called from the *Hausbuch* of Wolfegg Castle, a manuscript which contains humorous data about all sorts of curious objects. Though totally different from Schongauer, he also was one of the greatest engravers of the late fifteenth century. However, the roots of his style, in his rapidly executed, exquisite drawings (whether on paper or on copper) are to be found in the illuminated manuscripts of Holland. He is sometimes known as the Master of the Amsterdam Cabinet, since it is in Amsterdam that the greatest number of his prints are to be found.

Observe (Plate 31) in the realistic, ingenious, very Northern drawing by an anonymous Middle Rhenish artist an enchanting, vivid picture of a *Pair of Lovers.* They are captivating in their shyness, as they move forward with courtly ease. In the rendering of this incident from daily life there is a subtle suggestion of an over-ripe elegance. The exquisite drawing reflects the end of a wonderful, Northern era, rather than the prelude to a new epoch. You observe that the drawing is, in character, quite different from Schongauer's work (Plate 30). In his work we rarely find the realism that is striking here, with its vital originality of observation.

TITIAN

c.1477 · 1576

PORTRAIT OF A WOMAN

Uffizi, Florence

Plate 26

TINTORETTO

1518 · 1594

ARCHER

Uffizi, Florence

Plate 27

VERONESE

1528 · 1588

THE REST ON THE FLIGHT TO EGYPT

Fogg Museum of Art, Harvard University

Plate 28

TIEPOLO

1696 · 1770

THE REST ON THE FLIGHT INTO EGYPT

Fogg Museum of Art, Harvard University

Plate 29

SCHONGAUER

c.1445 · 1491

VIRGIN AND CHILD

State Museum, Berlin

Plate 30

MASTER OF THE HOUSE BOOK

Last quarter 15th century

PAIR OF LOVERS

Plate 31 *State Museum, Berlin*

DÜRER

1471 · 1528

SELF PORTRAIT

Albertina, Vienna

DÜRER

1471 · 1528

THE LAMENTATION

Fogg Museum of Art, Harvard University

Plate 33

DÜRER

1471 · 1528

PORTRAIT OF HIS MOTHER

State Museum, Berlin

Plate 34

GRÜNEWALD

c. 1455 · 1528

WOMAN WITH CLASPED HANDS

Oscar Reinhart, Switzerland

Plate 35

HANS BALDUNG GRIEN

c.1480? · 1545

THE THREE WITCHES

Albertina, Vienna

HOLBEIN THE YOUNGER

1497 · 1543

PORTRAIT OF JOHN FISHER

Royal Library, Windsor

Plate 37

JAN VAN EYCK

c.1390 · 1441

CARDINAL ALBERGATI

Dresden Gallery, Germany

Plate 38

LUCAS VAN LEYDEN

c.1494? · 1533

PORTRAIT OF A YOUNG WOMAN

State Museum, Weimar

Plate 39

BRUEGHEL THE ELDER

c.1520? · 1569

SELF PORTRAIT AND PATRON

Albertina, Vienna

BRUEGHEL THE ELDER

c.1520? · 1569

THE TEAM

Albertina, Vienna

DÜRER

1471 • 1528

Albrecht Dürer is akin to Leonardo in his restless intellectual curiosity. He is the most universal, the most balanced, and the greatest of all German artists of any period. His life is colored by his broad sympathies, his deep religious feeling, his love of nature, his scientific interests. As draughtsman, in any medium that he chose to use, he stands alone. He, Erasmus, and Luther were the leaders of the belated Renaissance in Northern Europe.

At the age of nineteen, Dürer started on a series of trips from his native city of Nuremberg. On the first journey he went to Colmar in the hope of meeting Schongauer, but he arrived too late. The famous Gothic master had died in 1491. In 1494 Dürer turned his steps to Italy where of all the artistic personalities of the day, Mantegna made the deepest impression upon him. In 1505 he undertook his second eventful trip to Italy, remaining in Venice for about two years. His art was now so widely and favorably known that he was looked upon as a master. He was profoundly impressed by the brilliance of Venetian art. At the end of two years he was loath to leave Venice for his native land, after so rich and profitable an experience in the South. Later foreign travel had a further effect upon his art. In 1520 he saw much of realistic painting in the Netherlands. All these foreign influences account, in part, for the increased breadth of his interests and of his achievements. He had become a versatile, sensitive personality. A heightened feeling for order, balance, rhythm and restraint, far in advance of that of his German contemporaries, marked his art. It was inevitable that he, in whose work there always lingered a substratum of the Gothic, should become the leader of the Renaissance in the North.

An understanding of Dürer's work must be based on a threefold approach:—a clear appreciation of the fact that the national characteristics of his art are in part rooted (Plate 33) in his sincere religious feeling; in part (see covers) on his profound love of nature; and in part (Plate 34) in his human warmth. Neither the Gothic fifteenth century artists who preceded him nor Holbein who followed him give proof, to the same extent, of these qualities. As a rarely gifted engraver and draughtsman we are not surprised to find that Dürer has left us impressive evidence of his preoccupations and interests, in black and white. The drawings by this universal genius (about one thousand in number) reveal in their wide range the fusion of these qualities. This we shall now see in a choice of only four masterpieces. We have in the *Self Portrait* (Plate 32) the rendering of the uneasy, tense face of a young genius. It is hard to believe that a boy of only thirteen years of age, working in the sensitive medium of silver point, which was new in Germany, should have been able to produce such a masterpiece, with so many striking features, such as the small, sensitive mouth and even the Mongolian-like eyes, a possible inheritance from his Hungarian ancestors.

The picture is still Gothic in the mode of presentation, although foreshadowing works of the Renaissance. Observe the absorption of the sitter, the animated hand with its pointing finger, the cast in the eye:—a portrait, in short, of a specific individual rather than of a type. And yet, in spite of these highly individualized elements, the total effect of the drawing, in its over-all aspect, is not yet of the Renaissance period. Because of its transitional elements on the one hand and because of its over-all Gothic exterior, on the other, there is little more than the premonition of a completely human, individual appeal which, when Dürer has become a fully developed and a more experienced artist, we shall find implicit in his Renaissance work.

The *Lamentation* (Plate 33), an impeccable masterpiece, once included in the splendid collection of the English painter, Sir Thomas Lawrence, is one of a group of drawings of Scenes from the Passion. I acquired it on a memorable night during World War I, while on leave in Paris, when, strange to record, most of those who attended the sale hesitated to bid on German art, even though produced four centuries earlier.

In its characteristic use of line, *The Lamentation*, so akin to woodcut in its total visual effect, seems to suggest that Dürer was, in the years 1521-23, contemplating another series of the Passion to be executed on wood. As a deeply religious person and a devoted adherent of Luther, Dürer repeatedly treated Scenes of the Passion—one of his favorite subjects. Such religious feeling is not only an individual but a national characteristic of Dürer's art. We find it in this wonderful pen and ink drawing in pristine condition.

By way of contrast, look at the water color and gouache, of 1503, known sometimes as *The Great Piece of Turf* or the *Grasses* (see covers) in which we have proof, as in many similar studies by Dürer, of his touching feeling for nature, of which it is one of a series of intimate studies. They are all of simple, everyday subjects, but masterpieces, one and all. Note the fascinating pattern in this closely observed tangle of grasses so lovingly rendered. Michelangelo, we are told, once said:—"Trifles make a masterpiece."

In *The Lamentation* (Plate 33) the rendering is far more emotional and less restrained than if it had been produced by an Italian. The German point of approach, in its various aspects, is illustrated first by Schongauer and then at the time of the Reformation by Dürer and Holbein. In Grünewald (Plate 35) and in Hans Baldung Grien (Plate 36) we shall find something similar, except that in their works the emotional note is less restrained.

But for the limitations of space it would repay us, in every instance, to put into simple words exactly what we see in each drawing, for obviously one of the elements that make us aware of the importance of a work of art is a full understanding of its subject matter. That, alas, we cannot do together in every instance. However, I do attempt it just once, at this point, to make clear what I mean and as a possible guide to the interested reader. The time and effort involved help us to make sure that we understand, not only the "Story," but also that we have observed with care all of the particular traits of each specific work of art, whether a painting or a drawing. So, in this instance, instead of merely pointing out the splendid rhythmic organization of the composition of *The Lamentation*, I prefer to push our inquiry further, for I remember the day, long ago, when a patient teacher said to me:—"Take your time and tell me exactly what you see." I thought, then, that to do so was a waste of time. Long practice in my own work, as in my teaching, has convinced me that the exercise is valuable and rewarding.

What then do we see in *The Lamentation?* At the foot of the cross a large group of ten figures. Below in the center Mary is seated at the side of Christ, embracing Him. We observe the crouching Magdalen to the right and to the left another holy woman. Among the standing figures Joseph of Arimathea, in the center, holds the winding sheet on which Christ lies. To the left we see a grief stricken woman, to the right St. Nicodemus carrying the jar of spices, and behind him an old man with a pointed hat. Farther to the right one of the Marys and St. John are represented, both with folded hands, and in the foreground the panel with the letters INRI, the crown of thorns, and the four nails.

If we are at all curious, we ask ourselves what is the source on which Dürer relied and from which he drew inspiration, for the Lamentation scene is not mentioned in the Bible. The origin of this scene dates from the mediaeval period and is first represented in Byzantine art, and in Italian paintings of the thirteenth century.

There are literary sources as well. We find an early mention in the so-called Meditations of St. Bonaventura:—"Joseph of Arimathea holds the winding sheet, Nicodemus brings the spices, Mary holds His head, kisses Him, and lays her hand in the bleeding one of Christ."

The tradition for this subject develops out of the Descent from the Cross as a special scene fitted for devotional purposes, with highly pathetic character. The High Gothic showed a trend toward a more emotional interpretation and for it there is a continuous tradition ever since the thirteenth century. The greatest early example is to be found in Giotto's fresco in the Arena Chapel at Padua.

While I said earlier that the drawing has certain characteristics in common with Dürer's mature woodcuts and that hence it might be looked upon as a preparatory study for a woodcut, I hasten to add that the drawing also shows tone effects more marked than the woodcut characteristics and may therefore be a quite independent drawing created for its own sake, instead of a preparatory study.

Finally, there are characteristics of the High Renaissance evident in this drawing, by which I mean:—its linear and sculptural character; its relief-like arrangement in parallel planes; and the tectonic character of the setting with horizontal and vertical accents dominating but with diagonals subordinated. Please observe that the light and shadow serve only to bring out the plastic clarity of the figures, and that while space and atmosphere are indicated they are still subordinated to the sculptural clarity of the figures.

If you will turn back for a moment and compare this Dürer *Lamentation* with Raphael's *Madonna* (Plate 25) you will observe in the Raphael a greater structural clarity, a larger rhythm of composition, a smoother, simpler flow of line, while in the Dürer *Lamentation*, with its lingering Gothic inheritance, we note a more twisted and crowded arrangement, a line that is more nervous, more restless, more ornamental, and an inner design and surface treatment that are richer but at the expense of the simplicity, the clarity and the monumentality of the Raphael.

This particular religious subject occupied Dürer's mind throughout his life. He varied the representations of it with great ingenuity. He does not accept the classic manner as a slavish follower, but develops that manner in his own way, avoiding settings that are too cold and too formal, by combining the monumental with the expressive quality of the German School.

This drawing which we have now looked at so closely, represents one of the most balanced compositions of its type in all of Dürer's work. It reveals, as we have seen, a strong emphasis on the religious and emotional content in a lively and clear setting. We have found inherent in it a beautiful graphic and ornamental quality, achieved through an unsurpassed mastery of sheer penmanship which, in its immediacy, is free and sensitive.

In the impeccable charcoal drawing of his dying *Mother* (Plate 34), done in 1514, we have one of Dürer's most candid, most impressive, most poignant, most unforgettable works:—an overpowering drawing of an aged, suffering woman. We are struck, first of all, by the severe and deep tragic quality, by the downright uncompromising definitions, by the complete avoidance of Italian idealization. It is a masterpiece of superb and vivid analysis, done with real warmth and Teutonic energy.

Dürer's portraits have, by this time, lost most of their purely Gothic character. They are now far more realistic, far more uncompromisingly penetrating than for instance in the early *Self Portrait*. I can think of no character drawing in all of Dürer's vast work (or for that matter in modern art) as deeply moving as the realistic picture of his Mother. Here we have proof positive, also, that in spite of his Venetian sojourn, he maintained unimpaired his national and his very personal German characteristics. The drawing of his Mother points the way to the expressionism of twentieth century German and North European art, as we see it in the work of Munch, the Norwegian, and his German followers, Nolde, Kirchner, Beckmann and others.

Dürer continued to the end a reverent student of the intimate aspects of nature. He made the exquisite drawing of Grasses in 1526, only two years before his death:— the same year in which he turned out some of his most famous portraits.

GRÜNEWALD

c. 1465* • 1528

In contrast to Dürer, the founder of the Northern Renaissance, Mathis Gothart Nithart, better known as Matthias Grünewald, was a mystic, an emotional expressionist, a precursor of the Baroque of the seven-

*See footnote 2, page 108.

teenth century. I select an example of his unique work because we have not the space to consider either Lucas Cranach, or the landscapists Altdorfer and Wolf Huber.

We must remember that expressionism and classicism are often merged in German art. In Grünewald's art the emotional content, the expressionist quality predominates.

By expressionism I mean an intense emotional striving by the artist to render his inner reactions to his subject with uninhibited emphasis. Grünewald's drawings (only thirty-six in number) are individual in style. They are in no way akin to an engraver's drawings. It has often been pointed out that Grünewald was one of the very few Germans who thought in terms of painting and all of his extant drawings are studies related to specific paintings. He never made drawings as preparations for engravings or woodcuts, or as works of art in their own independent right.

In the *Woman Beneath the Cross* (Plate 35),* as in his large, agitated and highly colored Isenheim Altar at Colmar, we are impressed by the artist's dramatic, passionate intensity; by his characteristic vehemence, brought about in part by the nervous action of the hands. There is little regard for formal beauty or for orderly arrangement, in the Renaissance sense. Even in the small reproduction of this large, animated, monumental drawing of about 1510 we seem to see the flickering, tremulous play of light over the entire surface, which adds to the effect of tension and excitement. Observe the use of parallel lines to give form

---

*See footnote 3, page 108.

to the head, bust and arms. Those lines serve to increase our awareness of an over-all tension. The anguish and emotional intensity are completely Teutonic and are enhanced by every other detail of the drawing—note the way Grünewald has drawn the shoulders, the clasped and twisted hands, and the unrestrained strands of dishevelled hair. The drawing is a study for the Virgin Mary of the Isenheim Altar.

HANS BALDUNG

c. 1480? • 1545

Hans Baldung Grien, apprenticed to Dürer for about two years, was one of the most imaginative artists of the first half of the sixteenth century. Dürer mentioned him in his will, which leads us to believe that he appreciated this independent artist of individual style who actually followed his master's example only in his distinguished woodcut work. Baldung made hundreds of drawings in addition to his paintings, woodcuts and designs for stained glass. The chiaroscuro drawing of the *Three Witches* (Plate 36), a mode he favored, illustrates clearly that he delighted in complicated movement, that he was more violent in expression than Dürer and that he, like Grünewald, is not unrelated to German expressionists of our time. He is more sensual in temperament than Dürer and while he produced portraits and religious pictures, he also delighted in representing erotic nude witches and beautiful female nudes who haunted the world of his imagination. In the choice of such subject matter he is a precursor of the Spaniard, Goya, centuries later.

HOLBEIN

1497 • 1543

The third and last genius among the German artists of the sixteenth century, Hans Holbein the Younger, whose greatest achievements are to be found in his analytical portraits, at seventeen years of age moved from his native city of Augsburg to Basel, where he became a citizen in 1520. Basel was an important center of the humanist school, and a center for the printing of books. In Basel he came in touch with Erasmus who commissioned him to make designs for title pages, so that the range of his activity was very wide, including the painting of frescoes for the town hall in Basel, the production of altarpieces as well as designs for stained glass and coats of arms. In such drawings he revealed his genius in the field of decorative art and ornamental design. His gift, in the early days, for representing the human figure in a rich architectural setting was marked. He made a trip to France and there got in touch with the Clouets and their technique of drawing portraits with colored chalk. However, he probably learned this technique from the Leonardo School during his earlier trip to Milan in 1519. In 1526 in order to escape the troubles of the Reformation he went to England, recommended by Erasmus to Sir Thomas More who, as his new patron, secured commissions for him and put him in touch with many people. In 1538 on a second trip to England he was appointed court painter to Henry VIII. Without his portraits of the king, his wives and the entourage at the court we would have a less authentic idea of the crafty king and the leading English personalities of the day.

The highly finished, black and colored *Self Portrait* (see covers), so akin to a painting, affords proof that Holbein was one of the master portrait painters of the sixteenth century, as well as the only draughtsman in Germany who takes rank alongside of Dürer. This *Self Portrait* was cut along the contours and colored with water color during a restoration. The face and hair were altered and gone over with colored chalk. Since Holbein tried this technique for the first time in 1523, in the *Head of the Leper* (a treasure of the Fogg Museum), but only mastered that technique fully in France, under the influence of Clouet, our *Self Portrait* may date from 1523 to 1524, when Holbein was 26 or 27 years old.

Holbein was a cosmopolitan, untrammelled by national traditions. He is far more modern to our eyes than Dürer and, therefore, seems nearer to our own world, for in his work there is no longer the lingering suggestion of the work of his Gothic predecessors. He is a realist who absorbed completely the lessons and the spirit of the Renaissance. We bracket his name with the great artists of the High Renaissance—Leonardo, Michelangelo, Raphael, Titian and Dürer. Holbein's portraits are essentially outline drawings rendered with amazing objective accuracy. In each portrait there is restraint coupled with intensity and penetration, in rendering the character that he paints or draws.

Not even the Clouets at the court of Francis I have left for the benefit of historians such extraordinarily vivid interpretations of famous characters, as for instance the analytical drawing of *John Fisher*, Bishop of Rochester (Plate 37). In no single one of Holbein's portraits is there a suggestion of a forced pose. In each instance we feel that the artist, by studied elimination presents only, and underlines in so doing, the character of his sitter. Indeed no truer likenesses were ever made at any other time or in any other country except perhaps in China. Most of these drawings are preparatory sketches for paintings and were made in one sitting. Subsequently Holbein produced the painting from the drawing at his leisure and according to a definite formula, as the Clouets did in France.

This noble portrait of John Fisher is a marvel of intuition. As we look at his features it is easy to believe the story about this old English bishop of eighty years who mounted the scaffold to go to his "wedding" as he called it. Holbein's guide in this, as in every other instance, was just the face of the sitter. Note the pale face, the thin determined lips, the nervous alert eye. Holbein has drawn for us an honest, determined old bishop.

In the presence of such a masterpiece, we are reminded of the words of Théophile Gautier, in which he asks us to stand in any of the great galleries before the portraits of Rembrandt and Holbein and look first upon the painted images and then upon the sightseers who pause before them and say which are the most living in your mind as distinguished from your eye.

IV

THE NETHERLANDS

IN CONTRAST TO ITALY, WE FIND THAT north of the Alps in the fifteenth and sixteenth centuries the mediaeval spirit still colors the appearance of drawings, as it does other works of art, even though the period is spoken of as the Renaissance.

In making a choice of drawings produced in the Netherlands, it seems best to go no further back than to Jan Van Eyck, in whose work we are confronted with a fully matured art which had its roots in earlier mediaeval miniature painting, produced at the courts of the Dukes of Berri and Burgundy. His art reflects a deep interest in individuality and in the world of reality.

VAN EYCK

c. 1390 • 1441

Jan Van Eyck and his brother Hubert (about 1370-1426), painters of the impressive Ghent Altarpiece, in which they used with striking effect the new oil technique, based their art on such illuminated manuscripts as the famous one produced by Pol de Limbourg for the Duc de Berri.

In the magnificent portrait of *Cardinal Albergati* (Plate 38), obviously a drawing done from life (a preparatory study for a less intimate and harder painting in Vienna), Van Eyck vitalizes for us the Papal Legate of great distinction who came to Flanders as a peace mediator between France and Burgundy. It alone, if there were no other evidence, offers irrefutable proof of his astounding capacity as a portraitist. Note the barely perceptible, restrained smile around the mouth; the keen, wise eyes; the lively end of the nose—all characteristic of a cultured human being of vast experience. Unnecessary details are subordinated. We have here a vital, unforgettable, rich personality.

Jan Van Eyck presents the Cardinal with subtle realism. His round bulk is monumental in its simplicity. The modelling, the texture, the surface of the face are amazingly subtle. In the linear method there is an absence of hard outlines. The effect is achieved through tonal values.

The mediaeval tradition of silver point was triumphantly carried forward in Flemish drawings of the fifteenth century. Such drawings are today almost unobtainable. A masterpiece of characterization such as that of Cardinal Albergati arrests our attention by a massiveness which we find in sculpture but which surprises us in so subtle a drawing. There is, in addition, a searching characterization of this particular man, who by some magic seems bathed in atmosphere.

BRUEGEL

c. 1520? • 1569

Peter Bruegel the Elder is a unique and original artist in the humanistic setting of sixteenth century Antwerp. In Bruegel's work there is no borrowing from Italian art, so usual in the Netherlands in the first half of the century; no classic balance; none of the formal beauty of the High Renaissance; no suggestion of Mannerism; no prelude to the coming Baroque style of Rubens in the next century. Bruegel, the greatest Flemish artist of his century, is the exception to the general rule. What he does anticipate is the realistic rendering of peasant scenes, the genre and landscape art of seventeenth century Holland. On his trip to Italy in 1552 his personality and point of view were uninfluenced by the work of Michelangelo and Titian.

Bruegel's paintings are better known than his drawings. He is, however, quite as much of a genius in his unconventional, original, genuine draughtsmanship, which often shows through the flat, transparent surfaces of his paintings. The surprising thing about his drawings, as his paintings, is their fresh vitality, their genuine simplicity, in contrast to the conventional, elaborate Mannerism of the period.

The robustly realistic, acutely observed, deeply original and witty drawing of the *Artist and Art Patron* (Plate 40)* is very close to life and yet in no sense photographic. It is done with delight in the two in-

*See footnote 4, page 108.

dividuals so tellingly depicted. It is probably a Self Portrait by Bruegel, with a patron. Note the marvellous combination of physical and spiritual values. Observe the penetrating eyes, the firm determined mouth of the artist, holding his brush, and then as a foil the very different, narrow eyes behind glasses, the enquiring nose, the thin, slightly parted lips of the close fisted patron. How effectively these contrasts and graphic comments bring out the whole story, even before we notice the whimsical final touch—the patron's right hand clutching his money bags.

The Team (Plate 41) is one of a group of figure studies bearing an inscription in Bruegel's own hand:— "after life"—by which he means taken from life as distinct from memory. This, again, is a vital drawing. So far as is known it was not used in either a painting or an engraving. It is done with Bruegel's usual accuracy of observation. He delights in the two horses and in the peasant—a national type. He draws this original, realistic picture with simplicity and with an expressive, sensitive outline.

• • •

In the seventeenth century the artists of the Netherlands are pre-eminent in Europe in the field of drawing as in engraving and etching. Before we proceed to look at a few examples of the work of the three giants of the century—Rubens, Van Dyck, and Rembrandt—I ask you to keep in mind the difference in religious belief of Holland and Flanders, for that fact is significant in its effect on the arts. To a large extent religious and political differences tend to explain the contrast between the exuberant art of Rubens and the aristocratic art of Van Dyck in Flanders, as against the more plebeian and homely art of Rembrandt in Holland. The Low Countries had changed from Burgundian rule to the Hapsburg Dynasty. With the coming of Charles V they passed under the rule of Spain. With extraordinary ability Charles V had controlled the unrest resulting from the Reformation. Under Philip II, his successor, the Dutch and Flemish people rose to defend their liberties. A bloody war followed and near its end very different roads were followed, clearly reflected in art. The Flemish provinces sided with the House of Hapsburg and the Catholic Church:—hence, in their art a continuance of a marked religious and aristocratic slant influenced by Italy. Of this Flemish-Catholic side, Rubens and Van Dyck are the outstanding exponents.

The Dutch provinces of the North, establishing their independence, became Protestant and Lutheran. Since their churches were not decorated with religious pictures as in the south, Dutch art developed along lay, domestic, intimate, plebeian lines. I stress this even though I am convinced that in many ways the scriptural works of Rembrandt (Plate 46) in their direct and intimate appeal are perhaps more truly religious, in the mediaeval sense, than are the creations of such Baroque artists of the Counter Reformation as Bernini, Ribera, and Rubens (Plate 42).

Rubens and Van Dyck stand revealed in their works as the commanding, sumptuous, prosperous, aristocratic artists of seventeenth century Flemish life; Rembrandt (and the host of followers whom we must pass over in silence) reveal in their works the simple, sober seventeenth century Protestant life of Holland.

RUBENS

1577 • 1640

Peter Paul Rubens, prince of Baroque painters, was a skillful diplomat who at times was entrusted with delicate peace missions between the Southern and Northern Netherlands and also between Spain and England. During his trip to Italy in 1600, and prior to his return to Flanders in 1608, he made copies of the works of Titian and studied the sculpturesque painting of Michelangelo. In this period he also produced some of his finest portraits at various princely Italian courts. He was a versatile genius who rivals in inventive faculty the great minds of the Italian Renaissance. He was a humanist and classical archaeologist, a sumptuous designer of religious, historical and allegorical canvases and a supreme master in pure landscape.

He has left us, in one of his finest drawings, a study for his famous religious canvas at Antwerp, the figure of Christ in the *Raising of the Cross* (Plate 42).

The soft crayon has modelled with power and subtlety and with a continuous rhythm a plastic figure of more than human vigor, swinging upward with superb energy. Rubens' concern for the perfection of details is demonstrated at the upper right corner, where with magic skill he has redrawn, in a separate study, the fleshy part of the tense thumb. In this typical and magnificent work, note the swelling lines that bound the contour, a beauty of line not unlike Raphael, combined with a power that we associate with Michelangelo.

By way of contrast, look now at the exquisite *Portrait of a Child* (Plate 43)* by our master. Observe the way the hair, the eyes, the tip of the nose and the mouth are drawn. Through the sure handling of these, Rubens has characterized the individual features of his son, Nicholas, in a superb study for an Infant Christ. There is in the portrait an absence of the classic restraint of the Renaissance. The details of the face are less sharply drawn than if done by an Italian Renaissance master. We have, instead, something warmer, in the brilliant rendering of the Child's mood.

VAN DYCK

1599 • 1641

Sir Anthony Van Dyck, the aristocrat, entered the busy studio of Rubens at fifteen and became his precocious pupil. Widely travelled, he was intensely industrious, vain, wealthy and independent. He was a gentler personality and far less exuberant than Rubens. He has to his credit many religious paintings, but throughout his short life, his best energy was devoted to the production of portraits, in large numbers, in which he has immortalized the Flemish, Spanish, French, Italian and English nobility, as well as his artist friends. He has left us in drawings and prints, as well as in paintings, a series of incisive, vivid, elegant portraits, full of romantic verve, of which not one is finer or more characteristic than the portrait of his art-

*See footnote 5, page 108.

ist friend, *Jan Snelling* (Plate 44), rendered with more than usual gusto.

You will observe in this picture that Van Dyck has rejected all that was not essential to his vivid interpretation of the sitter:—the total man as the world saw him. Van Dyck's artistic character is clearly revealed in pen and brush drawings such as this, produced brilliantly and rapidly. Our drawing is one of the studies for the famous *Iconographia*, a celebrated series of etched and engraved portraits of distinguished men, chiefly artists, completed prior to his visit to London in 1632 when he became court painter to Charles I.

I came to know this drawing well, many years ago, when under the friendly guidance of Mr. Thompson, I spent happy mornings in the library at Chatsworth and wonderful evenings in the living room with the Duke of Devonshire, poring over boxes of drawings with him and his family.

LUCAS VAN LEYDEN

c. 1494 ? • 1533

We couple the name of Lucas van Leyden, a prodigy who at sixteen was an accomplished engraver, with that of Dürer and Marcantonio, as one of the master engravers of the sixteenth century in Europe. They are the great triumvirate. Lucas lent distinction to the School of Leyden in the early sixteenth century, and as an engraver his work has at times been as popular as that of Dürer and is today highly prized by connoisseurs who value his exquisite technique.

The background of the drawing of the *Portrait of a Young Woman* (Plate 39) is restored. In its handling it already suggests the influence of Dürer, under whose spell Lucas fell when Dürer visited Antwerp. And yet, it is important to note the striking difference between the two artists, by turning back to look at the drawing of Dürer's *Mother* (Plate 34), done only a few years earlier than the Lucas portrait. What do we observe? Obviously the Lucas is far more restrained and static. In the Dürer there is much greater imaginative freedom in the revelation of character, in contrast to the Lucas in which only the outside aspect of the charming woman is effectively described. With his power for deep penetration, Dürer makes us realize the true nature, the true personality of his Mother. The static, rather sensitive but less imaginative Lucas head is characteristic of Dutch drawing of the early sixteenth century, in its simplicity, in its passive, solid, thoughtful character.

REMBRANDT

1606 • 1669

We come now to the inimitable, timeless art of Rembrandt van Rijn, master of mystery and characterization; a towering versatile genius and one of the giant draughtsmen of the centuries. The more intimate our knowledge of him, the deeper our conviction that in his drawings as in his prints he is unapproached and unapproachable. His drawings and his etchings discourage criticism.

Since no one has written of Rembrandt's art with more profound sympathy and understanding than Jakob Rosenberg, the sensitive connoisseur scholar, I am happy to quote a few telling sentences, in what follows, from his recent volumes on the master. Rosenberg is one of those rare teachers who can help us to "see." "Rembrandt," he says, ". . . was extremely productive in drawing motifs from daily life, although he painted very few such subjects. The charm of these sketches lies, in no small measure, in the artist's free and spontaneous reactions to the varied impressions he received at home or on the streets. Picturesque figures, characteristic gestures, all sorts of simple incidents caught his interest, and he speedily set them down on paper in his suggestive shorthand. This group of 'daily life' drawings is an impressive proof of the breadth and the vividness of Rembrandt's realism. It also reveals his unusual ability to absorb a vast amount of visual and artistic experience."

All this is perfectly illustrated in the masterpiece from the Morgan Library of *Saskia with her Child* (Plate 45). This is a vivid, exquisite sketch revealing keen observation in every detail. Note, for instance, the alert step down the stairs, the swaying body of Saskia, the gesture in her clasping arm and hand as she hugs her child, Rumbartus. And then note the marvellous relation between the two heads. We are held spellbound by this downright sincerity, this undeniable magic of draughtsmanship.

In presenting to you the very moving *Return of the Prodigal Son* (Plate 46), note these words of Rosenberg:—"We are often inclined to put freedom and spontaneity of execution above all other artistic qualities, and from this point of view, Rembrandt's drawing exerts a greater attraction than his painted work . . . The language of Rembrandt's drawing is surely more articulate and intimate, more immediate and more expressive than anything known in the seventeenth century, though this period did not lack genius in draughtsmanship. Rembrandt employed the art of drawing not only in the usual way, as a means of studying the visual world, of storing motifs, or preparing compositions for etching and painting. To him drawing became an art for its own sake, which allowed him to express his visions more speedily, yet no less articulately, than in any other technique. In the development of many of his favorite subjects which he created ever anew, Rembrandt's genius had a means of moving constantly along various paths. And it is in his drawings that we can best follow the inventive activity of his mind." Rosenberg calls attention to and helps us to appreciate "the artistic qualities of Rembrandt's draughtsmanship—its rare, electrifying vividness and suggestiveness, its extraordinary directness and pictorial sensitiveness." One fact is striking:—". . . the extraordinary preponderance of Bible subjects among the drawings. Most of these were obviously done not as preparatory sketches for paintings or etchings but as independent and complete works. And since the market value of drawings was negligible (in his time), they clearly manifest the artist's inner urge to deal constantly and intensely with religious subjects of the most varied sort."

Our moving drawing of the *Return of the Prodigal*

Son ". . . is the last, and perhaps the most profound manifestation of Rembrandt's religious attitude, symbolizing the forgiveness of God the Father toward weary and repentant man. Thus in choice as well as interpretation Rembrandt's biblical subjects reflect throughout his life his own experience and spiritual growth . . . Rembrandt interprets the Christian idea of mercy with the deepest solemnity, as though this were his spiritual testament to the world. The parable is Jesus's answer to the Pharisees who said: 'This man receiveth sinners and eateth with them' (Luke 15: 2); it is summed up in the words: 'I say unto you, that likewise joy shall be in heaven over one sinner that repenteth, more than over ninety-and-nine just persons, which need no repentance!' . . ." Our drawing, like the late great painting of the same subject in Leningrad, ". . . concentrates upon the act of forgiveness by the old father; his parental love and compassion dominate everything . . . What is meant and represented here is the divine love and mercy in its power to transform Death into Life. 'For this, my son, was dead and is alive again; he was lost and is found.' . . . The profoundly religious character of this late master work, and its great solemnity, seem to require a mediaeval cathedral rather than a baroque building as a proper setting."

The luminous drawing of a *View of London* with St. Paul's Cathedral, before the great London fire of 1666 (Plate 47), was probably an adaption by Rembrandt from some print or drawing and was made in his broad style about 1640 at the time that the master also copied prints of other English towns. Observe that character is achieved in this simple yet noble and powerful landscape through generous spacing and the suppression of useless detail. The drawing illustrates beautifully the master's success in rendering atmospheric effects and aerial perspective.

"Landscape," says Rosenberg, "was one of the most popular subjects in Dutch art. The naïveté and unpretentiousness, the pictorial sensitiveness and fidelity to nature of Holland's landscape painters have gained for them many friends in the course of the centuries; their reputation has risen to new heights whenever pictorial realism has been the prevailing trend. During the Baroque period in the Catholic countries, religious painting retained a dominant role. The royal courts of the day provided artists with countless commissions for the glorification of kings and princes. In Calvinistic and democratic Holland, however, both Church and Court had ceased to be influential patrons of the arts, and the innate love of the Dutch burghers for the intimate depiction of their surroundings gained free expression . . . Landscape subjects became increasingly popular, and the Dutch painters and etchers revelled in a detailed description of Holland's countryside. . . . it is a sign of Rembrandt's keenness and universality that he participated so actively in Dutch landscape art. But this he did in a very individual manner, for which no exact parallel can be found among his contemporaries. . . . He gained a conception of space in its most comprehensive aspect and learned in landscape work how to subordinate the individual form to a larger whole. . . . this phenomenon of daylight in the open air Rembrandt expressed most fully in his drawings and etchings. . . . Another impressive feature is the suggestion of air and atmosphere, which gains added significance as an element of pictorial animation. This Rembrandt achieved by his vibrant lines and tones, and by a subtly graded aerial perspective."

In his masterly landscape drawings he recalls to the mind's eye the work of the great Sung artists of China, by dispensing with all that is not essential. In the expressiveness and delicate balance of a few magic strokes he creates a vibrant, yet quiet air and a sense of distance. The character of Rembrandt's landscape drawing is beautifully illustrated in this particular example.

Rembrandt's studies of animals, like the famous *Lion* (Plate 48) of the Bonnat Collection in the Louvre, are astonishing. His amazing genius as a draughtsman is nowhere more strikingly manifested than in his sketches of animals. Many great masters of the past have been attracted by animals and have shown capacity in representing them; Pisanello (Plate 5), Leonardo (Plate 14), Dürer, Rubens and Delacroix (Plate 58). Rembrandt had no rival in his capacity to put on paper the essential characteristics of any living creature, whether the thick-skinned, lumbering elephant or a rapacious lioness.

Note how superbly the lion is here characterized. Observe the rendering of the relaxed beast; note the eyes that haunt and that tend to hypnotize us.

V

FRANCE

THE ART OF ITALY AND OF THE Netherlands exerted a profound influence on the artists of France. This is accounted for, to a certain extent, by the geographical position of France.

Let us begin our consideration of French drawings, which the writer has collected throughout his life with particular enthusiasm, by considering a brilliant example of the fifteenth century.

FOUQUET

C. 1420 • C. 1480

Jean Fouquet of Tours, one of the outstanding artists of Northern Europe in the fifteenth century, visited Italy and painted the Pope in Rome in 1447. Fouquet's style is Franco-Flemish and International in his many famous Illuminated Manuscripts, but in his powerful, sober portraits of equal renown, he is French, in spite of his debt to Jan Van Eyck.

One of the earliest pastels by any artist, of which we have a record, is the preparatory drawing (Plate 49) for the Louvre painting of *Guillaume Juvenal des Ursins*, who was Chancellor of France from 1445 until the death of Charles VII. He was a brother of the Archbishop of Reims and author of the history of Charles VI.

The mere notation of these few historic facts suggests that the sitter was a person of significance and capacity. How does Fouquet make him come to life in this serious, thoughtful picture of a man of rich and vital personality? How, in producing so weighty and so finely modelled a head, has he revealed this versatile, well-poised, intensely human personality of assured position? We are struck immediately by the fact that Fouquet has rendered the character of the worldly-wise historian and politician with sober realism. We see him in absorbed yet slyly attentive, observant mood. We note his introspective eyes, his thin upper and fleshy lower lip, his heavy jowls, his inquisitive nose —all in all a self-assured, shrewd personality. Nothing diverts us from our interest in this massive head. *Juvenal des Ursins* is rendered with masterly skill and simplicity. We are grateful that no decorative details distract our attention from this unforgettable head. We carry away the lasting impression of a self-assured, tranquil, impressive personality—very real and pulsating with life. If we compare the drawing with that of *Cardinal Albergati* (Plate 38), we see at once that Fouquet is indeed indebted to Jan Van Eyck. In these two vital heads of real persons there is a similar calm, a similar monumental simplicity, a similar emphasis on texture and, above all, deep insight.

In the presence of this drawing, the astute general

observation of Théophile Gautier (page 61) is pertinent, once again.

CLOUET

before 1520 • 1572

Black and red chalk drawings constitute the glory of French art in the sixteenth century. They represent one of the two artistic currents of the time, well illustrated by the portrait of an *Unknown Man* (Plate 50) by François Clouet, acquired during World War I from the collection of the Marquis de Biron, then occupying the spacious house on the Rue de Varennes, Paris, that is now the Rodin Museum. The Marquis spent his last years in exile in Geneva, where I visited him again after the War, surrounded by his superb collection of Italian eighteenth century drawings by Tiepolo, Canaletto and Guardi, many of which today grace the important collection of drawings of the Metropolitan Museum, New York.

The fashion for the type of Clouet drawing here illustrated is due to Catherine de' Medici who in the sixteenth century patronized and kept in close touch with Clouet, her official painter. Very different in style and purpose were the works of the Italian decorators also employed at the court of Francis I. The Italians brought to France the classical spirit which pervaded all Europe.

The career of François Clouet shows interesting parallels and contrasts to that of the Italian decorator, Primaticcio, his contemporary at the court of France.

Both were of foreign blood, the former of Flemish parentage, the latter of Italian birth. Both won fame and high position under Francis I, Clouet as portrait painter to the king, Primaticcio as director and designer of the royal scheme of decoration. Both maintained their supremacy under Henry II and Francis II, and, until they died, under Charles IX.

Clouet amplified and refined the art of his father, Jean, as Primaticcio, who belonged to the Raphaelesque tradition, did the style of his predecessor, Il Rosso. After dominating the art of their time, both initiated powerful trends which persisted well into the seventeenth century. It is striking to observe two such utterly divergent artistic ideals as those expressed in Franco-Flemish portraiture and in Italian decoration surviving side by side, fostered by the same court, yet neither encroaching upon the other for over one hundred years. The two traditions, however, may be said to have common characteristics which can be traced to the presence of the two artists at the French court. These are a subtle quality of style and a certain fastidiousness of approach and of design.

It is fascinating and instructive to remember that the sixteenth century portrait painter followed no such trying procedure as that of the present day with its innumerable sittings and inevitable changes of mood. François Clouet at the court of Francis I, and Hans Holbein the Younger at the court of Henry VIII, asked the subject to give one sitting at which, with sure and telling strokes, a black chalk drawing such as this was made. Subsequently the artist, at his leisure, produced a painting according to a definite formula.

An amazing number of portrait drawings of the sixteenth century have survived as a result of the fashion popularized by Catherine de' Medici of forming portrait albums of important men and women of the time. Many of the drawings are copies, frequently of excellent quality, after such originals as the one that we reproduce.

RUBENS

1577 · 1640

RAISING OF THE CROSS

Fogg Museum of Art, Harvard University

Plate 42

RUBENS

1577 · 1640

A STUDY FOR AN INFANT CHRIST

Albertina, Vienna

VAN DYCK

1599 · 1641

PORTRAIT OF JAN SNELLING

Chatsworth, England

Plate 44

REMBRANDT

1606 · 1669

SASKIA WITH HER CHILD

Pierpont Morgan Library, New York

Plate 45

REMBRANDT
1606 · 1669

THE RETURN
OF THE
PRODIGAL SON

Teyler Museum,
Haarlem

REMBRANDT
1606 · 1669

VIEW OF
LONDON WITH
ST. PAUL'S
CATHEDRAL

State Museum, Berlin

REMBRANDT
1606 · 1669

A LION
Louvre, Paris

FOUQUET

c.1420 · c.1480

PORTRAIT OF JUVENAL DES URSINS

State Museum, Berlin

Plate 49

FRANÇOIS CLOUET

Before 1520? · 1572

PORTRAIT OF AN UNKNOWN MAN

Fogg Museum of Art, Harvard University

Plate 50

POUSSIN

c.1594 · 1665

MEDORO AND ANGELICA

Plate 51 *Museum of Stockholm, Sweden*

CLAUDE LORRAIN

1600 · 1682

LANDSCAPE WITH TREE

Christ Church, Oxford

Plate 52

WATTEAU

1684 · 1721

THREE STUDIES OF A NEGRO'S HEAD

Louvre, Paris

Plate 53

FRAGONARD

1732 · 1806

THE CONFIDENCE

Boymans Museum, Rotterdam

Plate 54

INGRES

1780 · 1867

PORTRAIT OF PAGANINI

Bonnat Museum, Bayonne

Plate 55

INGRES

1780 · 1867

STUDIES FOR THE GOLDEN AGE

Fogg Museum of Art, Harvard University

Plate 56

GERICAULT

1791 · 1824

NEGRO SOLDIER HOLDING A LANCE

Fogg Museum of Art, Harvard University

Plate 57

POUSSIN

c. 1594 • 1665

We call attention next to a very fine, apparently simple drawing by the restrained Nicolas Poussin, scholar and outstanding master of the style of seventeenth century French "classicism" in painting, who, with Claude, a more lyrical singer, was one of the two notable French landscape painters patronized by Popes and Cardinals. Poussin and Claude exerted a profound influence on the art of France, even though both settled in Rome and spent a large part of their lives in Italy where they were subject to the influence of their Roman contemporaries. Throughout his life Poussin fell under the spell of antique art as well as of its myths; also under the spell of Titian and other Venetians. Both his classic interests and his love of nature are reflected in the drawing of *Medoro and Angelica* (Plate 51), set in a typical, luminous landscape.

Medoro, a humble Moorish youth of great beauty, was wounded and Angelica nursed him, fell in love with him, and married him. They lived at Cathay where, in right of his wife, Medoro became king. In Ariosto's *Orlando Furioso* we learn this was the cause of Orlando's madness.

Poussin strove throughout his life to capture order and unity in even the slightest of his productions. His inspiration for these he found in the antique, in architecture and in sculpture, as in the works of Raphael and other Renaissance masters in Italy, adapting what he studied to his own personal uses, by adding chiaroscuro effects to give depth even to his sketches, as to the rhythms of his more ambitious canvases, for which such sketches were preparations. Appreciation of Poussin's controlled, calm paintings is impossible without an understanding of his swift shorthand but carefully planned drawings suffused with light. His peopled landscape sketches are no longer conceived as mere backdrops for his paintings, as earlier masters had used landscape.

CLAUDE

1600 • 1682

Poussin's friend, Claude Lorrain, the companion of Northern landscape painters resident in Italy, in a wash drawing like the admirable study of a *Tree* (Plate 52), expresses even more than in his paintings the very essence of his art. Long before the Venetians, the medium of pen and wash had been mastered by him and by Poussin to render space, atmosphere, depth, distance and effective contrasts of light and shade. Claude thus anticipated, by two centuries, many of Corot's ideas in France and Turner's in England.

Although no landscape painting of Claude's is known which bears a date earlier than 1631, his fame was well established before that date and the distinguished patronage of successive Popes and Cardinals had already begun. Today he is more widely known and praised for his landscape drawings than for his paintings. Those who limit themselves to a study of Claude's paintings are likely to fall into the error of believing him conventional, theatrical, and lacking in reality. They tend to admire only his poetic sense of space composition and his use of light as a central illuminating and stylistic motif. In his sketches Claude is far less stilted. He reveals in all of them a rare gift to create the illusion of atmosphere, to represent nature realistically. For years he spent all the daylight hours watching the changing effects of light and air over the Roman Campagna. His drawings, which are usually in warm, deep tones, sometimes heightened with white, are often direct studies from nature. "Their spaciousness, quiet and sunlit calm are expressive of the beauty and dignity of a lost Arcadian world, envisioned with the northerner's longing for antique lands." Technically they display a power to compose in terms of grand simplicity, a mastery of wash which has seldom if ever been equalled, and a poetic sensitivity to atmospheric effects which is rivalled only by the Chinese. An incomparable collection of Claude's drawings is in the British Museum and in the Louvre. The famous *Liber Veritatis*, which it was thrilling to study years ago in the collection of the Duke of Devonshire at Chatsworth, contains over two hundred drawings kept by Claude as a record of the pictures he had painted, for even in his own lifetime his paintings were imitated and forged.

WATTEAU

1684 • 1721

Let us turn now to the enjoyment of the preparatory drawings for scenes of festive love-making which the

French appropriately term "fêtes galantes," a designation for the new and refined amusements of Parisian society of the day. In the eighteenth century France once again assumed leadership in art and culture, ushering in a gayer style in revolt against the formal elements of the previous century—the classicism of Charles LeBrun and his Academy. The eighteenth century, internationally viewed, is, indeed, the French century. Its finest exponents were Watteau, Boucher, and Fragonard. The spirit of the early years of the century is triumphantly summed up in Jean Antoine Watteau's greatest painting, *The Embarkation for Cythera*, (the island of Aphrodite's birth), about which Austin Dobson wrote the following rondeau:—

"After Watteau"

"Embarquons-nous!"[1] I seem to go
  Against my will. 'Neath alleys low
I bend, and hear across the air—
  Across the stream—faint music rare,—
Whose "cornemuse,"[2] whose "chalumeau?"[3]

Hark! was not that a laugh I know?
  Who was it, hurrying, turned to show
The galley swinging by the stair?—
  "Embarquons-nous!"

The silk sail flaps, light breezes blow,
  Frail laces flutter, satins flow;

[1]Let us set sail
[2]bagpipe
[3]flute

You, with the love knot in your hair,
You will not? Press her, then, Pierrot,—
"Allons,[1] embarquons pour Cythere;"
"Embarquons-nous!"

Watteau was born in Belgium. The roots of his art stem from Holland and Flanders and not from the art of the classicist Poussin or the Academy, but rather from Rubens and Titian. He spent most of his brief creative years in Paris, where he died at the age of thirty-seven. For a proper understanding of his paintings, a study of his drawings is mandatory. Let us, then, consider together the work of this melancholy poet-painter in two of his astonishingly sensitive drawings. A reasonable number of these exquisite masterpieces offer proof that he was interested in Oriental and racial types, as in the famous example of *Three Studies of a Negro's Head* (Plate 53). No later hand has retouched this beautiful drawing of great brilliance. I was under-bidder on this drawing at the Max Bonn sale in London. Unfortunately, I lost it to the fabulous collector David-Weill of Paris, having earlier in that sale acquired the so-called *Leper* by Holbein—to secure which I had crossed the Atlantic, reaching Sotheby's sale room in the nick of time. Such are the fortunes of war among collectors.

In *Three Studies of a Negro's Head*, as in all the drawings of Watteau, we are thrilled by the magic of the most distinguished draughtsman of his century—one of the finest and most sensitive of any epoch. Wat-

[1]Let us go

teau confessed that he delighted more in drawing than in painting. He crowded his notebooks with studies of all kinds—copies from old masters, *Nude Female Figures* (see covers), heads, hands and feet, ladies in taffeta, soldiers, actors, gallants, children, animals and landscapes. He sketched—with telling accents on every ear, mouth, tip of nose or chin—his servants and his friends, the latter often dressed in fantastic costumes which he had collected and in which his friends good-humoredly posed. Out of the separate studies in the sketch books he chose and arranged the figures or groups of figures that he wished for his painted compositions.

The melancholy consumptive, working sometimes eagerly and even feverishly through the brief fifteen years of his artistic maturity, never failed in the sharpness of his observation. The exquisiteness of his taste, the sensitivity of his temperament and the dexterity of his touch gave to his least crayon sketch a distinction and a grace which have caused even his slight drawings to be treasured by every collector of discernment since his own time. At once decisive and delicate, subtle yet firm, they express the essence of the French court of the eighteenth century. Like other pages of similar studies, the sheet of *Three Studies of a Negro's Head* served him in his painting.

I may possibly exaggerate the exceptional mastery and charm of the *Nude Female Figure* (see covers) because as a boy, on my first visit to the Louvre, I tried to copy the transcendently delicate rendering of the half-length graceful nude, with its subtle combination of characteristics—emphatic accents and a soft caressing line. I struggled in vain to capture the enticing contour of her back through the use of that sensitive line which gives roundness to the form.

In considering Dürer's *Lamentation* (Plate 33), we found that in understanding the subject matter of the drawing, our appreciation of its merits was definitely enhanced. In Watteau's *Nude Female Figure*, the subject matter is so obvious that it requires no interpretation to make its meaning clear. To appreciate, however, what captivates the eye, is nonetheless of importance in grasping its merits as a work of art, namely:—that the seductive figure is represented as a logically consistent whole. There is unity here and masterly emphasis through the telling placement of every accent. The presence of these important elements, which transcend the reporting of facts as the camera might give them, is what makes Watteau's work of art a great master drawing.

Jean Seznec, the brilliant literary historian, said in a recent address with some of these very drawings in mind to illustrate his poetic thought:—"Sometimes the literary historian is at a loss to express, in a condensed formula, the dominant characteristic of a period, its mood, its unique complexity; he feels that any successive definition will be hopelessly inadequate; then he turns to drawing—and there it is: the quintessence of a society, of its moral physiognomy, of its temper, of its taste, revealed at a glance in the profile of a Clouet crayon (Plate 50), in the curve of a woman's arm in a sanguine by Watteau (see covers), in a few strokes of pen and brush by Tiepolo (Plate 29), in a frantic arabesque by Delacroix (Plate 58)—the fragile epitome of a civilization, the signature of a century."

Drawings like the two by Watteau carry a message that no words can convey. Could feminine grace be more adroitly rendered or a momentary attitude caught with greater perfection than in his *Nude Female Figure* (see covers)? Observe how perfectly bust, arms, hands and fingertips are delineated. Watteau has no superior in grace. Who has ever better represented (Plate 53) the most appealing side of the black man? Who has more closely observed him? And yet the personality of Watteau lurks in every line. There is in such sketches of Negroes a certain subtle sadness, characteristic of Watteau himself, although he is known to the superficial observer as the supreme painter of eighteenth century gaiety, the master of idyllic painting.

BOUCHER

1703 • 1770

François Boucher's *Reclining Nude* (see covers), with its carefree, exuberant and yet dainty, piquant elegance, is the perfect reflection of the taste of his times. He is the facile painter of voluptuous women, in whose work Post sees "a subtle fusion of adolescence with a fully developed feminine type."

The favorite of Mme. de Pompadour, and popular with the entire court, Boucher was ceaselessly employed in painting for his sophisticated patrons of the fashionable world countless decorative panels and mythological pictures such as the one for which this drawing is a study. His drawings, produced with astonishing ease, represent in their fantasy, grace and fair coloring the best of the French Rococo. Boucher, who also was occupied with designs for the tapestry weavers at the royal establishments at Beauvais and Gobelins, for porcelain manufacturers at Vincennes and Sèvres, was the first to consider drawings as more than studies to be put away in portfolios. The elegant ladies of Louis XV court were quick to accept his point of view and sought after his drawings as they did his paintings and his illustrated books. His drawings reveal an unfailing sense of composition, a rich fancy and a rhythmical, graceful line. The drawing of a *Reclining Nude* ought to be reproduced in its original, beautifully carved Louis XV frame.

There is no finer or more thoroughly characteristic extant example by the master, which, thanks to the generosity of John Nicholas Brown, once more graces the Fogg Museum Collection. I say "once more" because I had acquired it with conviction and enthusiasm in my youth and then, on submitting my French drawings to the senior member of the department, the late Dr. Denman Ross, an astute collector of his generation, whose words were law in those far-off days, he generously approved of all the drawings except this, one of the most prized of my possessions, saying that the proportions of the graceful figure were incorrect. With lack of independence, but with a heavy heart, I let it go. In the years that followed, during which I secretly longed for its return, Berenson's words about Botticelli's *Abundance* seemed to apply in this instance as well:—". . . In many of the world's great masterpieces it is wiser to discount at a glance such failings as all may discern and devote ourselves if we are able to wooing the indwelling soul of the beauty." And then, after more than a decade, my generous pupil, Brown, brought it back into the fold.

FRAGONARD

1732 • 1806

We close our consideration of the drawings of the Rococo period in the final years of the reign of Louis XV with the work of Boucher's pupil, vital, frivolous, hot-blooded Jean Honoré Fragonard, an ardent lover of fêtes. He was born eleven years after the death of Watteau in the perfume-laden, brilliant sunlight of southern France, at Grasse. Of all the sophisticated eighteenth century artists it was he who was the born painter and draughtsman. Precocious at 18, he already helped Boucher on the cartoons for his tapestry commissions. The true quality of Fragonard's genius we must look for in his drawings. It is in them, influenced as they are by the example of Tiepolo far more than by Rembrandt, that he is most spontaneous. Only Watteau surpassed Fragonard in recording with the crayon or the brush the momentary charm of pose or gesture, done in a broad, impressionistic manner. He stands, as it were, midway between his two great predecessors, Watteau and Boucher, lacking the intangible pathos of the one and the occasional vulgarity of the other, but recording more fully than either, with more gaiety, greater luminosity, and often with more license, the temper of the Rococo period. In *The Confidence* (Plate 54), he reveals a love of feminine elegance and grace akin to Watteau's, but it is an exterior comment, with no haunting expression in the eyes and no mobility in the mouth or fingertips.

We have, in these few drawings by Watteau, Boucher and Fragonard, had a glimpse of the charm of the Rococo period in France. Watteau, the brooding dreamer, initiated the movement early in the century. Fragonard, the Provençal, returning to Paris in 1761 with the Abbé de Saint-Non, with whom he had travelled in Italy, carried on the development of the movement with gusto for years, in the service of financiers and people of the stage, until the French Revolution and the authority of David's neo-classic style—which he had always abhorred—drove him, sorrowing, back to his cousin's home in Grasse. He returned to Paris once more, however, under the official protection of David, and died, almost forgotten, in 1806.

• • •

The many gifted artists of the nineteenth century in France were well aware of the important achievements of the past in Europe, for they haunted the museums, as has always been the habit of the best creative artists.

In a brilliant article written by Professor Meyer Schapiro of Columbia University for *An Introduction to Contemporary Civilization in the West*, he enlarges on the fact that "the development of modern painting was not in a straight or single line," and he proceeds to make clear that "no period in the history of art was more conscious of its past than the XIX Century . . . The absence of the older atelier system with its rigid practices; the lack of religious enthusiasm; the discredit into which an unproductive academic manner had fallen, the free facilities of travel, the easy access to museums and books, all these were factors in the creation of a more personal style on the part of the artists of the XIX Century. Thus the painting of the century does not illustrate a gradual evolution of one style, but shows a series of creative efforts by *individuals*, whose work diverges in different directions from existing forms and produces a medley of counter currents. Although to a certain extent influenced by the work of men immediately preceding them, the painters of the XIX Century depended even more on a remoter past. The art of the century is an intensely personal art."

The influence of *David*, art dictator and leader of the neo-classic movement, pervaded the academic art schools. Reactions were inevitable, and led, as we shall see, in the time of the Romantics, to an emphasis on Mediaeval and Renaissance models in literature as in art.

INGRES

1780 • 1867

The outstanding exponent of David's teaching, particularly in the field of portraiture, was Jean Auguste Dominique Ingres, in whom however, the effect of neo-classic tyranny was modified by romantic longing and by a study of Raphael. Ingres wrote in his prime:— "My enthusiasms remain what they always have been, Raphael and his century; the ancients, and above all the divine Greeks; in music Gluck, Mozart and Haydn."

The late Bryson Burroughs once said:—"No modern has approached Ingres in his ability to express substance and character by a grandly synthesized line, unless it be his own follower Degas. Ingres was never wholly successful in rendering emotion, nor did he seem able to coordinate his more ambitious works into a unified whole. His less elaborate compositions with their quieter poses, and his portrait drawings are, therefore, the most satisfactory."

The kind of immortality, which, as we have seen, Holbein and Clouet achieved for the courtiers of Henry VIII and Francis I, and Van Dyck for the artists and aristocrats of Flanders, Ingres gave in the nineteenth century to a sober, bourgeois world. In his pencil portraits he united a fastidious line with exquisite characterization. It is the rare combination of subtle intuition, skillfully minute delineation, and fidelity to appearance which gives his drawings their special character and charm—a charm not unlike that of the characters in the novels of Jane Austen. His portraits, like the one of the musician *Paganini* (Plate 55),* are accounts of the outer rather than the inner man. The emphasis is upon those assured aspects of life and fortune which are shown to the world. Through clarity, precision, and balance these serene pencil portraits achieve distinction without, however, the penetration of the great sixteenth century masters. *Paganini*, in the Louvre, is presented calmly, clearly without a trace of the kind of romantic passion that characterizes the superb oil sketch of this same musician by Delacroix, in the Duncan Phillips collection, Washington, D. C.

The universal present day interest in the portrait drawings by Ingres makes many collectors and stu-

---

*See footnote 6, page 108.

dents lose sight of the high significance of the large number of equally notable drawings of nudes, perfectly illustrated in one of the master's studies for his painting of the *Golden Age* (Plate 56), left to the Fogg Museum by Grenville Winthrop, the greatest American collector of nineteenth century drawings in our time. Note how through a process of elimination and balance, the contours of the sides of the beautiful nudes are rendered in subtle correspondence. In drawings of this type we see the influence on Ingres of his passionate interest in Greek sculpture and vase painting.

My understanding of *quality* I owe fully as much to Martin Mower, a gifted teacher, as to my fellow collectors and to my colleagues in the scholarly world.

One of these, Carl Dreyfus, Curator at the Louvre, took me to see his father, Gustave Dreyfus (1837-1914), a true "amateur" in the eyes of the French, who at 35 years was the owner of a veritable little museum. His remarkable collection of Renaissance sculpture and medals, acquired in about 1870 to 1872 and now a glory of the National Gallery, Washington, was in the old days housed in overcrowded rooms. Some years later, Dreyfus introduced me to his father's life-long friend, the Director of the Ecole des Beaux Arts, the French painter, Leon Bonnat, whose fashionable portraits brought him contemporary fame and riches, enabling him, from 1875 on, to become the most discriminating and princely collector, in Paris, of master drawings.

Every collector is, I believe, stimulated to adventure into new fields by contact with an older, more experienced and enthusiastic collector. My own deep interest in the work of Ingres is the outgrowth of a study of some of his finest drawings in the Paris studio of Bonnat. I visited him frequently almost up to the time of his death at over ninety years. In his spacious studio in Paris, with a military cap of 1870 always on his head, he continued to paint until the end, converting the funds that he received from the sale of his canvases into the permanent worth of Great Drawings. Most of the treasures which he gathered during a long lifetime are now beautifully housed in the museum of his native city, Bayonne; others, like the Paganini, he bequeathed to the Louvre. Like the majority of real connoisseurs, he put into the privacy of his living rooms the drawings he cared for most of all. Even his bedroom was adorned with the works of Ingres and on either side of his shaving mirror and on every wall there were distinguished examples by Ingres.

GERICAULT

1791 • 1824

Theodore Gericault was an ardent, independent, indefatigable enthusiast of very catholic taste, whose admiration for the masters of the past was as deep and genuine as it was broad. Rubens, Rembrandt, the Venetians and particularly Michelangelo were the heroes of this first of the French Romantics. Gericault studied and understood the frescoes of Michelangelo in the Sistine Chapel, adapting the lessons he learned to his own needs in depicting contemporary subject matter, such as horses in the *Riderless Races at Rome* and in his enormous canvas of the *Raft of the Medusa*, a complicated report of a much publicized shipwreck.

Gericault and Delacroix, with their interests in current happenings, both revolted against the neo-classicism of David. They were the outstanding exponents of the Romantic Movement, turning from Greek and Roman legends and history to contemporary events, as well as to subjects of mediaeval literature or oriental life. They infused their pictures with a sense of greater reality, with an enhanced liveliness. In their drawings, the line employed by the Romantics appeared more accidental, less wiry, and less clearly defined. The person represented in our spirited drawing of a *Negro Soldier* was probably Gericault's model, Joseph (Plate 57), in an Egyptian costume. Gericault had many costumes, collected on his travels in North Africa. In these he dressed his models. In the light of such technical mastery and such originality, for his time, in the choice of subject matter, one wonders what he might have produced had he lived beyond his early thirties. Even so the drawings, like the paintings and lithographs of this first of the fiery spirits of the romantic revolution, show a vigor of execution which was new in French art and pointed the way for succeeding generations in France.

DELACROIX

1798 · 1863

AN ARAB RIDER ATTACKED BY A LION

Fogg Museum of Art, Harvard University

Plate 58

COROT

1796 · 1875

PORTRAIT OF "FLORE"

British Museum, London

Plate 59

COROT
1796 · 1875

VIEW OF
MT. SORACTE

Fogg Museum of Art, Harvard University

MILLET

1814 · 1875

MME. SENSIER

Fogg Museum of Art, Harvard University

Plate 61

DAUMIER
1808 · 1879

THE SOUP

Louvre, Paris

DEGAS

1834 · 1917

MME. HERTEL

Fogg Museum of Art, Harvard University

Plate 63

DEGAS

1834 • 1917

A BALLET DANCER

Fogg Museum of Art, Harvard University

Plate 64

GOYA

1746 · 1828

TWO PRISONERS IN IRONS

Plate 65 *Metropolitan Museum of Art, New York*

DELACROIX

1798 • 1863

Eugene Delacroix, an individualist, benefited by his companionship with Gericault. Highly intelligent, well read, and inventive, he was to lead the Romantics after Gericault's untimely death, in a further development of the new point of view. Literature, mediaeval history as well as current happenings, offered tempting subject matter to Delacroix. Dante, Shakespeare, Goethe, Victor Hugo, Byron and Walter Scott all stimulated his creative imagination. However, he never slavishly followed the text of his favorite authors. In his brilliant paintings his color is based on a study of Rubens and the Venetians. From the English painter Constable he also learned new possibilities in landscape and in the use of color.

In most of his drawings, as in his paintings, Delacroix thinks of the composition as a whole rather than of the various parts. This is perfectly illustrated in the *Arab Rider Attacked by a Lion* (Plate 58). Such drawings reflect his pictorial ideas expressed in a nervous draughtsmanship of rhythmic accents, broken contours and dramatic emphasis. Delacroix depicts force and struggle. In his drawings there is hurried movement and superhuman strength. His line, unlike the cool line of Ingres, betrays his emotion as he attempts to recreate the rich and changing visions of his imagination. The artistic forebears of his style were the Baroque painters of seventeenth century Flanders, but the splendor and noble sentiment of Rubens's talent are not equalled by Delacroix. More than that, he could not rival Rubens either in the command of form or in his conception of space.

In the spirited drawing of the *Arab Rider Attacked by a Lion*, inspired by an incident witnessed on his trip to Morocco, we are struck first of all by the constantly interweaving pattern of the design, by a complete lack of formalism. The drawing illustrates also Delacroix's taste for the strange and the exotic.

COROT

1796 • 1875

As elder statesman, so to speak, Camille Corot, a lovable, simple personality, has usually been associated with the Barbizon School of landscape painters. His well composed, quiet work delights us by its note of poetic distinction. We tend to forget his amazing gifts in painting and in drawing the nude and his capacity in rendering a draped figure. Observe in the thoughtful, sober *Portrait of "Flore"* (Plate 59) how free it is from all calligraphic tricks. We are struck in this figure, reminiscent of Italy, by the pervasive mood of tranquillity which characterizes the sitter and also by the marked plasticity of form, unusual in an artist who was not primarily sculptural in his work. It is one of the very great drawings of its type in the nineteenth century. Nothing is neglected that makes for a completely satisfying and convincing rendering. I was underbidder for the drawing at a sale in London, but lost it to the connoisseur-scholar, Arthur M. Hind, who added it to the vast treasure of the British Museum.

Turning now to the other and very different Corot drawing, of superlative quality, the *View of Mt. Soracte* (Plate 60), which, if there were no other evidence, offers triumphant proof of the master's astonishing capacity as an observer and as a draughtsman of landscape; as sensitive as Claude to the effects of light and like Poussin, a master of design.

"Mt. Soracte, a limestone ridge rising majestically out of the campagna north of Rome, has been a source of inspiration to poets as well as painters. Byron describing the Apennines wrote:—

> I've looked on Ida with a Trojan's eye;
> Athos, Olympus, Aetna, Atlas, made
> These hills seem things of lesser dignity,
> All, save the lone Soracte's height, displayed
> Not *now* in snow, which asks the lyric Roman's aid
> For our remembrance, and from out the plain
> Heaves like a long swept wave about to break,
> And on the curl hangs pausing.

"Note the depth and vibrancy of atmosphere in our drawing, a grandeur and sweep which stem from the 'Great Tradition' of both poetry and painting—in its breadth and organization and in its emphasis on the noble aspects of nature."

MILLET

1814 • 1875

It is natural to think of Jean François Millet as a painter devoted solely to the life of the stolid peasant in the scenes of his daily labor in the field or in the home. An intimate, highly individualized likeness such as that of *Mme. Sensier* (Plate 61), probably done at Barbizon in the early fifties, makes it clear that he was also a nineteenth century portraitist whose method is based on the great French tradition of sixteenth century pencil and red chalk drawing, in a combination of force and subtlety, simplicity of technique and understanding of character. Mme. Sensier is here characterized with distinction in a drawing, that is impressive in its bulk. Note the dome-like forehead and the curiously lively eyes, which give the face its special character. During the years of his early struggle Millet did a series of portrait drawings, which he sold for a few francs. After 1848 he only occasionally did this type of work. In the presence of our notable picture one regrets that Millet's portrait drawings have largely disappeared. Mme. Sensier was the wife of the critic, landlord, biographer and devoted admirer of Millet.

DAUMIER

1808 • 1879

We come next to another one of the master artists of the nineteenth century, one of the most personal of French draughtsmen, the illustrator and caustic cartoonist, Honoré Daumier, who studied the work of Michelangelo and Rembrandt. From the former he learned construction of massive form, and from the latter dramatic intensity through the pictorial and emotional device of chiaroscuro. All this is triumphantly illustrated in our forceful drawing of *The Soup* (Plate 62), which tells its story so clearly that no comment in mere words is necessary. Where else, in the nineteenth century, will you find such convincing human realism? Nowhere else, and indeed only, if we look back to Rembrandt in a picture like *The Prodigal Son* (Plate 46), or to Goya in a drawing like the *Two Prisoners in Irons* (Plate 65), do we find a similar dramatic use of light and shade to render emotion.

Daumier witnessed much of the activity of Ingres, the classic, and that of Gericault, Delacroix and the other Romantics. He was practically a contemporary of the realist Courbet and of the lyrical singer, Corot. Manet passed from the scene only a few years after Daumier's death. The Impressionists, and the Individualists—Degas and Cézanne—had already given the world some of their best work when Daumier died.

During his full life, in spite of the artistic currents that swirled around him, Daumier remained unperturbed and created with marked independence and consistency well over three thousand lithographs for *Caricature* and the daily paper *Charivari* (most of which I have collected in Paris since boyhood) as well as a thousand woodcuts and countless drawings and paintings. No other draughtsman has ever left for the student of human nature so many priceless records of a passing epoch; no novelist has ever mirrored for posterity a more throbbing, varied world. The medium of lithography proved a perfect vehicle for the notation of his telling satire and was more freely used by him than even by his Spanish predecessor, the first romantic artist, *Francisco Goya* (1746-1828), (Plate 65). Observe the sharp contrasts of light and shade which play over the broken surfaces of the Goya. The pathetic figures of the *Two Prisoners in Irons* stand firmly and immovable in brilliant light. With apparently simple means they are tellingly rendered and with a reality that is, says Agnes Mongan ". . . more vivid than nature . . . It is man suffering, bewildered, and abandoned, tortured and torturing. There are no mere arabesques or felicitous contours in this grim tale. Every brief and brutal stroke expresses the maximum of tragedy or hopeless yearning, with light and darkness always playing an important role, one of double significance."

Goya, famous as portrait painter of Spanish aristocrats, was also profoundly sensitive to the sufferings of humanity, and particularly after a serious sickness in 1792 expressed his biting satire in a style that while based on Rembrandt is quite his own. If he had never painted, but had left us only his drawings and his aquatints, with their impassioned condemnation of war, inspired by the attack instigated by Bonaparte against Charles IV of Spain—they alone would afford proof that Goya, precursor of the Romantic movement in France, was the greatest Spanish artist of the period. It is a strange fact that he remained a court favorite in spite of his vitriolic satire in lampooning the vices of the court. We have digressed to speak of Goya, in order to call attention to the influence of such work on Daumier.

And now returning to Daumier let us stress the point that no man was ever more "of his time" than Daumier. No man who ever lived was more of a translator of life into contemporary, everyday terms by means of masterly drawing. Although the themes for his satire are frequently earthy and commonplace, as in *The Soup* (Plate 62), all that he depicts is rendered in the grand style; everything is drawn, in an elemental way, worthy of Rembrandt. Note in this drawing how the swelling lines of varying width reveal, in magic fashion, a Michelangelesque solidity of form.

Daumier may be compared in the field of graphic art to the novelist, Dickens. They are both city men who observe and record with rare insight the daily life, the varying emotions and activities of the everyday man. Daumier possesses the astonishing ability of Dickens to make his individuals stand for types. Daumier, however, pushes his ridicule of bourgeois society farther than Dickens. Daumier, the satirist, like Dickens also lampoons contemporary abuses in politics, in business, in the legal profession, and does so with vitriolic gusto. We need not read the captions underneath his pictures to understand the story which he tells so clearly and convincingly. Even though his caustic drawings may be of only passing or local interest, there is in each one something elemental, almost titanic in its style. His ability to depict through facial expression—punctuated by the emphasis of gesture—fleeting and conflicting human emotions is unequalled. In the whole field of art there are no finer examples than those by Daumier of drawing from memory. "I considered in what various ways," he said, "and to what different purposes the memory might be applied and fell upon one which I found suitable to my situation and idle disposition—laying it down first as an axiom that he who could, by any means, acquire and retain in his *memory* perfect ideas of the subjects he meant to draw, should have as clear a knowledge of the figure as a man who can write freely hath, of the twenty-four letters of the alphabet and their infinite combinations. By repeating in my own mind the parts of which objects were composed, I could by degrees combine them and put them down with my pencil. Thus I formed the early habit of retaining in my mind's eye, without coldly copying it on the spot, whatever I intended to imitate." With such a point of view, held with such deep conviction, Daumier rebelled in his youth against the academic restraints of the ordinary art school and sought his models in every part of Paris including the Louvre. Balzac said these true words about Daumier's drawing:—"Here is a fellow who has Michelangelo under his skin."

DEGAS

1834 • 1917

My enthusiasm for Edgar Degas was shared by my friend, the late connoisseur-scholar, Henri Focillon, a French teacher of renown in Paris, as well as at Yale University and at Harvard's Dumbarton Oaks, Washington.

We agreed that if we could choose but one example it would have to be the impeccable drawing of *Mme. Hertel* (Plate 63), a preparatory study for the painting in the Havemeyer Bequest, a treasure of the Metropolitan Museum, New York. We tried to analyze this preference and found that it was due to the fact that this wistful drawing seemed to us to illustrate perfectly the superb capacity of Degas as a draughtsman; the artist's vital imagination and visualization of actuality; a triumph of French taste, a "sensibility" quite absent in many of the finest drawings by Ingres. Here Degas has depicted gesture with keen observation. We agreed that the master had always recorded gesture and movements which were the result of and reflected fixed habits, associated with particular professions and the exertions characteristic of his varied models—his relatives and friends, ballet girls, shop girls, laundresses, jockeys or others. We were baffled by the ingenuity of an artist who, with such economy of means, could render *Mme. Hertel* with those qualities of French charm and repose which set their stamp of time, place, station and nationality upon the sitter. If you will look at the reproduction (Plate 63) a little more closely you will observe that Degas merely indicated the pose of her body. His attention was concentrated upon the face, with its curious eyes and the ghost of a smile and upon the intensely personal gesture of the expressive and beautifully drawn hand. This drawing, made in 1865, shows clearly Degas' debt to Ingres, a master for whom he had during the whole course of his life the deepest admiration. Degas studied Ingres' portrait drawings with concentration, and also collected them, as he did those of Delacroix, Corot and other masters. In his hand, however, the pencil, as you observe, had more freedom and moved with easier rhythms than in the hand of Ingres. Moreover, the intelligence that guided it was more subtle, more probing and more original, so that Degas' drawings show a greater variety and suppleness of pose, a more immediate and personal interpretation of character. In contrast to Ingres' contained and solid people, Degas' are presented with an informality which, because of the perfect balance of his taste and judgement, in no way detracts from their distinction but reveals characters of more pulsating life.

In the *Ballet Dancer* (Plate 64) Degas has again depicted gesture with remarkable skill. The drawing is a study for a figure in the background of the *Rehearsal for Ballet on the Stage*, of which there are two versions in the Metropolitan Museum, New York. Technically the drawing is doubly interesting. Degas had already, by 1872, adopted the use of colored papers, in this particular case not dissimilar in tone and texture to certain prepared pink papers of the Florentine fifteenth century. He has not yet abandoned the pencil, but he strengthens the contours with a rich black crayon. It can be debated whether it was failing sight—caused by the injury to his eyes from night sentry duty during the war of 1870 and the Commune—or whether it was the natural development of his style which led him gradually to abandon pencil on white paper in favor of crayon and then pastel. With these he drew larger, fuller forms, freer contours, and more diverse movements.

Royal Cortissoz, until his death a few years ago, was the beloved art critic of the New York Herald Tribune, a lifelong student of drawings and a passionate collector of reproductions. He repeatedly pointed out that in his opinion Degas was, like Ingres, a miraculous craftsman, with a passion for rectitude of drawing. He was right in thinking that this passion for "rectitude of drawing" was the thing above all others that explained Degas' devotion to the old masters.

Degas, as a practising artist, haunted the museums and in his drawings paid tribute to the great Florentines and other masters of the past. He reverently copied many of the old masters—Mantegna, Holbein, the Clouets and many others—and thus emphasized his respect for good precedent. This accounts for the dignity of his representations no matter how commonplace or even vulgar his models happen to be in the course of his career. We should learn from his example that great originality may go hand in hand with a profound respect for tradition. We ought also to ponder the fact that to the very end of his long and industrious life he continued, in the field of art, to be a tolerant, open-minded and understanding collector of works produced by those late nineteenth and twentieth century artists, a selection of whose drawings, did space permit, ought to be included in any group of Great Drawings.

I shall never forget the scene when the heirs of Degas saw fit in the memorable summer of 1918, a year after the master's death, to dispose of, at an auction which I attended, all the paintings, drawings and lithographs that were left in his studio. One session of the sale was held on a memorable night during World War I. The Fogg drawings, here reproduced, were among those that came up for sale. The auction room was filled with French officers, men on leave, and agents of the Government, who by their presence, at such a time, testified to their passionate interest in art. They bid on pictures and drawings at a time when the fate of their nation was at stake. During the sale one could hear the German guns in Paris, when very few people realized that American troops had won their first real success of the war at Château-Thierry.

ERRATA

[1] Credit on Plate 16 should read *Royal Library, Turin.*
[2] Date on Plate 35 should read 1465.
[3] Title on Plate 35 should read *Woman Beneath the Cross.*
[4] Title on Plate 40 should read *Artist and Art Patron.*
[5] Title on Plate 43 should read *Portrait of a Child.*
[6] Credit on Plate 55 should read *Louvre, Paris.*

RECOMMENDED READING

BENESCH, OTTO. *Rembrandt: Selected Drawings.* London, New York: Oxford University Press (Phaidon Press), 1947. 2 v. (Text and plates.)

BENESCH, OTTO. *Venetian Drawings of the Eighteenth Century in America.* New York: Bittner, 1947. (Bittner art monographs.)

BERENSON, BERNARD. *The Drawings of the Florentine Painters.* University of Chicago Press, 1938. Amplified edition. 3 v. (Text, catalogue, illustrations.)

Fundamental work on Italian drawings.

BLUNT, ANTHONY. *The French Drawings in the Collection of His Majesty the King at Windsor Castle.* London, New York: Oxford University Press (Phaidon Press), 1945.

BRITISH MUSEUM. *A Handbook to the Drawings and Water-colours in the Department of Prints and Drawings,* by A. E. Popham. London, 1939.

The best of the modern handbooks on drawings in English.

BUFFALO FINE ARTS ACADEMY. *Master Drawings, Selected from the Museums and Private Collections of America.* Buffalo, 1935.

CHICAGO ART INSTITUTE. *Drawings, Old and New,* compiled by Carl O. Schniewind. The Art Institute of Chicago, 1946.

CLARK, KENNETH. *A Catalogue of the Drawings of Leonardo da Vinci in the Collection of His Majesty the King at Windsor Castle.* Cambridge, England: University Press, 1935. 2 v. (Text and plates.)

DELEN, A. J. J. *Flemish Master Drawings of the Seventeenth Century.* New York: Harper, 1950.

DE TOLNAY, CHARLES. *History and Technique of Old Master Drawings, a Handbook.* New York: Bittner, 1943.

DODGSON, CAMPBELL. *Modern Drawings.* London, New York: Studio Publications, 1933.

EDE, H. S. *Florentine Drawings of the Quattrocento.* New York: McBride, 1926. (Drawings of the great masters.)

FRANKFURTER, ALFRED. *Master Drawings of the Renaissance.* Art News Annual, XXXVII, (1939), pp. 97-117.

GETTENS, R. J. AND STOUT, G. L. *Painting Materials: A Short Encyclopedia.* New York: Van Nostrand, 1942.

GOMBRICH, E. H. *The Story of Art.* London, New York: Oxford University Press (Phaidon Press), 1950.

Admirable. Recommended for careful reading.

GRADMANN, ERWIN. *French Master Drawings of the Eighteenth Century.* New York: Harper, 1949.

HARVARD UNIVERSITY, FOGG MUSEUM OF ART. *Drawings by Agnes Mongan and Paul J. Sachs.* Cambridge: Harvard University Press, 1946. 2 v. (Text and plates.)

HARVARD UNIVERSITY, FOGG MUSEUM OF ART. *One Hundred Master Drawings,* edited by Agnes Mongan. Cambridge: Harvard University Press, 1949.

Winslow Ames contributed to this volume a valuable simplified account of the terms used in describing the materials of drawings.

HOLME, BRYAN. *Master Drawings.* New York, London: Studio Publications, 1943.

KIMBALL, S. F. *Great Paintings in America; One Hundred and One Masterpieces in Color,* selected and interpreted by Fiske Kimball and Lionello Venturi. New York: Coward-McCann, 1948.

LOZOWICH, LOUIS. *A Treasury of Drawings, from Pre-history to the Present.* New York: Lear, 1948.

LUCAS, E. L. *Books on Art, a Foundation List.* Cambridge: Fogg Museum of Art, Harvard University, 1938.

MEDER, JOSEPH. *Die Handzeichnung; ihre Technik und Entwicklung.* 2° aufl. Wien: Schroll, 1923.

The only non-English text listed, but fundamental for serious study.

MELLAART, J. H. J. *Dutch Drawings of the Seventeenth Century.* New York: McBride, 1926. (Drawings of the great masters.)

MIDDELDORF, U. A. *Raphael's Drawings.* New York: Bittner, 1945.

MUCHALL-VIEBROOK, T. W. *Flemish Drawings of the Seventeenth Century.* New York: McBride, 1926. (Drawings of the great masters.)

NEW YORK. METROPOLITAN MUSEUM OF ART. *European Draw-*

ings. New York: 1942. v. 1, Italian drawings. v. 2, Flemish, Dutch, German, Spanish, French and British drawings.

New York. Museum of Modern Art. *Modern Drawings,* edited by Monroe Wheeler. New York, 1944.

Oxford University. Ashmolean Museum. *Catalogue of the Collection of Drawings,* by K. T. Parker. Oxford: Clarendon Press, 1938. v. 1, Netherlandish, German, French and Spanish schools.

Panofsky, Erwin. *Albrecht Dürer.* 3rd edition. Princeton University Press, 1948.

Parker, K. T. *The Drawings of Antoine Watteau.* London: Batsford, 1931.

Parker, K. T. *The Drawings of Hans Holbein in the Collection of His Majesty the King at Windsor Castle.* London, New York: Oxford University Press (Phaidon Press), 1945.

Parker, K. T. *Drawings of the Early German Schools.* New York: McBride, 1926. (Drawings of the great masters.)

Parker, K. T. *North Italian Drawings of the Quattrocento.* London: Benn, 1927. (Drawings of the great masters.)

Pope, Arthur. *The Language of Drawing and Painting.* Cambridge: Harvard University Press, 1949.

Popham, A. E. *The Drawings of Leonardo da Vinci.* New York: Reynal and Hitchcock, 1945.

Popham, A. E. *Drawings of the Early Flemish School.* New York: McBride, 1926. (Drawings of the great masters.)

Popham, A. E. and Philip Pouncey. *Italian Drawings in the Department of Prints and Drawings in the British Museum, the XIV and XV centuries.* London: 1950. 2 v.

Popham, A. E. *The Italian Drawings of the XV and XVI Centuries in the Collection of His Majesty the King at Windsor Castle,* by A. E. Popham and Johannes Wilde. London, New York: Oxford University Press (Phaidon Press), 1949.

Puyvelde, Leo van. *The Dutch Drawings in the Collection of His Majesty the King at Windsor Castle.* London, New York: Oxford University Press (Phaidon Press), 1944.

Puyvelde, Leo van. *The Flemish Drawings in the Collection*

of His Majesty the King at Windsor Castle. London, New York: Oxford University Press (Phaidon Press), 1942.

REGTEREN ALTENA, J. Q. VAN. *Dutch Master Drawings of the Seventeenth Century*. New York: Harper, 1949.

ROSENBERG, JAKOB. *Rembrandt*. Cambridge: Harvard University Press, 1948. 2 v. (Text and plates.)

SAN FRANCISCO GOLDEN GATE INTERNATIONAL EXPOSITION. *Master Drawings, an Exhibition of Drawings from American Museums and Private Collections*, arranged by Annemarie Henle. San Francisco: 1940.

SHOOLMAN, R. L. *Six Centuries of French Master Drawings in America*, by Regina Shoolman and Charles E. Slatkin. New York: Oxford University Press, 1950.

SUTTON, DENYS. *French Drawings of the Eighteenth Century*. London: Pleiades Books, 1949.

TAYLOR, F. H. *The Taste of Angels, a History of Art Collecting from Rameses to Napoleon*. Boston: Little, Brown, 1948.

TIETZE, HANS. *The Drawings of the Venetian Painters in the 15th and 16th Centuries*, by Hans Tietze and E. Tietze-Conrat. New York: Augustin, 1944.

TIETZE, HANS. *European Master Drawings in the United States*. New York: Augustin, 1947.

TIETZE, HANS. *Tintoretto: The Paintings and Drawings*. London, New York: Oxford University Press (Phaidon Press), 1948.

TIETZE, HANS. *Titian: Paintings and Drawings*. London, New York: Oxford University Press (Phaidon Press), 1937.

VASARI, GIORGIO. *Vasari's Lives of the Artists: Biographies of the most Eminent Architects, Painters, and Sculptors of Italy*, abridged and edited by Betty Burroughs. New York: Simon and Schuster, 1946.

Excellent reproductions are available in such series as the Albertina Facsimiles, and in publications of the Marées-gesellschaft, the Prestel-gesellschaft and the Vasari Society.